THE SECOND DOCTOR WHO QUIZ BOOK

Also by Nigel Robinson

The Doctor Who Quiz Book
The Doctor Who Crossword Book

THE SECOND DOCTOR WHO QUIZ BOOK

Compiled by
Nigel Robinson

A TARGET BOOK
published by
the Paperback Division of
W. H. ALLEN & Co. Ltd

A Target Book
Published in 1983
By the Paperback Division of
W. H. Allen & Co. Ltd
A Howard & Wyndham Company
44 Hill Street, London W1X 8LB

Reprinted 1984

Printed and bound in Great Britain by
Anchor Brendon Limited, Tiptree, Essex

ISBN 0 426 193504

CONTENTS

The Answers

THE QUESTIONS

1. Name the Doctor's favourite planet.
2. Which two members of the TARDIS crew have been knighted?
3. Upon impending break-up, the TARDIS has a fail-safe mechanism. What is the effect of this mechanism and in which adventure was it brought into use?
4. By what name is Sol Three in Mutters Spiral better known?
5. Name the Black Guardian's servant in (a) *The Armageddon Factor*; (b) *Mawdryn Undead*; (c) *Enlightenment*.
6. Which alien race has two hearts, a temperature of 60° Fahrenheit and a breathing rate of four breaths a minute?
7. Who was (a) Arak in *Planet of the Spiders;* (b) Eirak in *Terminus*?
8. Every TARDIS is equipped with a chameleon circuit enabling it to disguise itself to blend in with its surroundings. Whose TARDISes have disguised themselves as (a) a fireplace and a Concorde; (b) an ionic column and a sedan chair; (c) a block of ice and a motorbike?
9. Each of the three TARDISes mentioned above has at one time or another disguised itself as a London police box. Give the reasons in each case.
10. What is hyper-space?
11. In which constellation is Gallifrey?
12. The TARDIS travels in the fourth and fifth dimensions. Time is the fourth dimension. What is the fifth dimension?
13. Martian society is sharply divided into two castes: the Ice Warriors and the Ice Lords. Name the three Ice Lords encountered by the Doctor.
14. Whose ship was (a) *The Black Albatross*; (b) *The Shadow*; (c) *The Annabelle*?
15. Who were the Dals?
16. What is a Time Ram?

17. Earth is the third planet out from its sun. Which planet is the twelfth out from its sun?
18. Identify the following planets; (a) the levels of radiation on it were so high that its population had to retreat underground; (b) it was made into a giant space museum; (c) it was used as a prison planet where convicts were put to work in the tinclavic mines; (d) it is sixty thousand light years away from Earth; (e) it was an Earth colony in the year 2020.
19. What is the only force known to chield anti-matter?
20. What is a Tissue Compression Eliminator?

The Adventures of the First Doctor/1

1. On which planet was the Space Museum to be found?
2. In *The Ark*, we were witness to the final destrection of the Earth as it plumetted into the Sun. When did this take place?
3. The Zarbi were originally a placid and mindless species living in co-existence with the Menoptera. What had changed them into the deadly creatures encountered by the Doctor, Ian, Barbara and Vicki?
4. What was the planet of Giants?
5. How long had the pilot of flight Red-Fifty been imprisoned by the Mechonoids?
6. Where exactly did the TARDIS carrying the Doctor and Dodo land in 1966?
7. Who was Diomede?
8. Ian fell victim to the 'plague' which had swept the Sensorites' planet. Why were the other members of the TARDIS crew unaffected?
9. How were the Menoptera armed?
10. Which member of the TARDIS crew was found guilty of the murder of Eprin in the city of Millenius? Who had actually done the deed?
11. Whose summer palace was to be found at Shang-Tu?
12. Why did the Princess Joanna threaten to have the Pope excommunicate her brother, King Richard the Lion-heart?

13. Most sentient life forms, it seems, are dependent on an atmosphere similar to our own. Which creatures encountered by the Doctor breathed an atmosphere composed largely of ammonia?
14. Which planet was turned in a matter of minutes from a lush if deadly jungle world to a dust planet?
15. When the TARDIS landed in the Kalahari Desert, the crew was witness to a battle between which two legendary warriors?
16. The escape chain with which the time travellers became involved in revolution-torn France had been infiltrated by a traitor. Name him.
17. Who 'paid for their sins and lost on the draw'?
18. Whom did Zentos suspect the Doctor, Steven and Dodo to be when the TARDIS first materialised on board the Space Ark?
19. What is the fate of those who play the Celestial Toymaker's games and lose?
20. How did the Doctor strand the Meddling Monk (a) in 11th century Northumbria; (b) on an ice planet?

Adventures in History/1

1. What brought about the creation of the Universe?
2. What brought about life on Earth?
3. According to Susan, what is the Doctor's favourite period of Earth history?
4. Name the four survivors of the ship which foundered on Fang Rock during the Rutan's attack on that islet.
5. Which chinese magician played at the Palace Theatre in the late 19th century?
6. In the last adventure of his second incarnation the Doctor remarked to Jamie and Zoe that the TARDIS had materialised at one of the most terrible times in the history of Earth. Where had they landed?
7. The Highlanders were the supporters of which Scottish prince?
8. Whom did the Doctor meet in the Garden of the Aged in 15th-century Mexico?

9. Name the father of Hur.
10. James Stirling was a master spy who led an escape chain during the French Revolution. What secret identity did he assume in France?
11. Why did Poppea, the wife of Nero, order Barbara's death?
12. For whose treasure was Samuel Pike searching?
13. Name the Marshalls of Tombstone and Dodge City at the time of the Doctor's visit to the Wild West.
14. A coward by nature, the Meddling Monk decided to reverse his plans and help the Vikings in their battle with King Harold. With what weapon did he intend to provide them?
15. Who was Haroun ed Diin? Why did he bear such a great hatred towards El Akir?
16. Where was the TARDIS crew imprisoned by the Tribe of Gum when the time machine materialised in prehistoric times? Who released them? Why?
17. Who was Richard Mace?
18. What was the Day of Darkness?
19. Who introduced firearms to the Middle Ages?
20. Name the ancient Atlantean who was brought forward in time to the present day by Professor Thascales.

The Adventures of the Second Doctor/1

1. The second Doctor often consulted his well-thumbed diary. What period of years did this journal cover?
2. Where did the TARDIS materialise in the year 2020?
3. What was ECCO?
4. How did the TARDIS crew escape from the Great Intelligence when it trapped them in space?
5. Why did the Krotons come to the planet of the Gonds?
6. On which planet were (a) the Issigri mines; (b) the Clancey mines?
7. Name the managing director of International Electromatics.
8. The removal of the TARDIS's space/time element will cause the time machine to break up. This nearly happened in *Terminus* before the fail-safe mechanism

came into operation. In which adventure did the TARDIS actually break up to leave the Doctor and his companions floating in space?

9. Who was used as Yeti bait in Tibet?
10. Name the Highlander who escorted the Doctor and his friends back to the glen near Culloden where the TARDIS had materialised.
11. On what did the Macra live?
12. It is now well known that the Doctor, being a Time Lord, has two hearts. Which other alien race, encountered by the second Doctor, also has two hearts?
13. Who was Penley?
14. Why did Edward Travers come to Tibet?
15. To prove to Jamie that he was in full control of the TARDIS the Doctor set the co-ordinates for Mars. Needless to say, the time machine did not reach the Red Planet. Where did it materialise?
16. Who was Nurse Pinto?
17. Who gave the War Lord and his people the technology to travel through time and space?
18. Name the two Dominators who came to the planet Dulkis.
19. Whose spacecraft was the LIZ 79?
20. How did the Doctor succeed in transporting himself, the Brigadier and Sergeant Benton to Omega's world?

The Daleks and the Thals/1

1. Both Davros and the Doctor saw the Daleks as being a force for good. In what manner?
2. The Doctor first met the Thal race in *The Daleks*. When did he next meet them?
3. Name the leader of the resistance group against the Daleks in (a) *The Dalek Invasion of Earth*; (b) *Day of the Daleks*.
4. Who nearly became the very first victim of a Dalek? Who saved him?
5. Who were the three named members of the Movellan expeditionary force to Skaro?

6. After the centuries-long great war, and the development of the Daleks from the Kaled race, what happened to the Thals?

7. In the flight from the Pursuer Daleks in *The Chase*, the TARDIS materialised in several locations. Name three of them.

8. Which member of the Daleks' Grand Alliance of the 41st century represented the largest galaxy?

9. Two members of the Earth expedition to Exxilon had particular reasons for hating the Daleks. Who were they, and what were their reasons?

10. The Daleks' supreme weapon of the 41st century, the Time Destructor, was powered by one emm of taranium which had been mined on Uranus. How long had it taken to mine the emm of taranium?

11. Name the brother of Ganatus.

12. How did the first Doctor and his friends succeed in immobilising a Dalek in their city on Skaro?

13. The Robomen received their orders from the Daleks via their helmets. What would have happened to a Roboman were his helmet to have been removed?

14. Of what metal is the outer casing of a Dalek made?

15. The Daleks originally came to Spiridon to use its icecanos to deep freeze their vast army. Why and how were they forced to modify this plan?

16. Who did the Kaleds first suspect the Doctor and Harry to be?

17. After arriving on Skaro, Barbara complained of a headache, something from which she very rarely suffered. What was the cause of her headache?

18. Name the Governor of the Vulcan colony which was threatened by the Daleks.

19. When the second Doctor met the Daleks on Vulcan, the creatures seemed to recognise him instantly from their previous encounters. How did the Daleks discover the Time Lord's identity in *Day of the Daleks*?

20. Confronted by hostile robomen on the banks of the Thames in 2164, the Doctor and Ian decided to swim for it, only to be confronted by a Dalek rising out of the water. On which planet did a Dalek arise in a similar fashion from the sand?

1. To which hospital was the Doctor admitted when the Time Lords exiled him to Earth?
2. At what alien form of self-defence was the third Doctor particularly adept?
3. Who was Moni?
4. No crops grew on Exarius. Why?
5. What did Professor Horner believe the barrow at Devil's End to contain? What did it really contain?
6. A colony of some twenty Drashigs were to be found in circuit five of Vorg's Miniscope. Where did the Drashigs originate?
7. Who was Varan?
8. Name Professor Thascales' two assistants at Cambridge.
9. Who attempted to destroy the royal citadel of Peladon with a sonic cannon?
10. Between which two great galactic empires was the Frontier in Space?
11. What are the special properties of Axonite?
12. What was so unusual about the core of the planet Spiridon?
13. Who was Cliff Jones?
14. Who was the Great One?
15. Seriously injured after his escape from the Ogrons' planet, how was the Doctor able to pursue the Daleks through space to Spiridon?
16. How did Governor George Trenchard meet his death?
17. The Doctor and Jo travelled to Auderley House to investigate Sir Reginald Styles's seeing a ghost. What had the diplomat seen in reality?
18. Arriving on Peladon for the second time, the Doctor was accused by Orton of being a spy. Who confirmed the Doctor's true identity as a friend of Peladon?
19. What solution did the Doctor foresee in the conflict betwen the Humans and the Silurians?
20. Which alien creature has a natural affinity with plastics?

1. How many days' journey from Earth was Monarch's ship when the TARDIS landed there?
2. Who finally destroyed BOSS and ended its plans for world domination?
3. Why was Sir Reginald Styles obliged to make an emergency flight to Peking?
4. Which Silurian was in favour of negotiations with the Humans? How did he die?
5. The Fendahl skull was found in which country on Earth?
6. When did the Krynoid pods arrive on Earth?
7. The countdown to the Third World War, initiated by Hilda Winters and Professor Kettlewell, was halted by the Doctor. How was the countdown stopped when the Giant Robot set it into operation?
8. How did the hand of Eldrad reach Earth?
9. Which alien race twice became the conquerors of Earth, in each instance to be defeated by the Doctor?
10. How many War Machines did WOTAN have built?
11. What were the visible effects of the Great Intelligence's return to Earth?
12. How were the Yeti armed when they invaded Central London?
13. Name the Deputy Security Commissioner for Europe and North Africa who was discredited and dismissed by Salamander.
14. Who was the second in command of the North Sea oil refinery who took over its running after John Robson had become infected by the Weed Creature?
15. How did the Ice Warriors transport their deadly seed pods to Earth?
16. How did the army under Colonel Lethbridge-Stewart attempt to halt the advance of the Great Intelligence's Web?
17. How did the Terileptils plan to rid Earth of its inhabitants?

18. Returning to London from the Middle Ages, the Doctor and Sarah Jane found the city under martial law. Name the military commander of the capital.
19. Where was the seat of government in Britain during the dinosaur invasion?
20. How were the Silurians at Wenley Moor finally defeated?

Companions of the Doctor/1

1. Identify these companions of the Doctor; (a) she regarded the Doctor as almost as clever as herself; (b) she considered using the Doctor as a case history in her thesis; (c) she was the secretary of an eminent scientist; (d) she was offered the chance to start a new life on the planet Skaro; (e) the 'mouth on legs'.
2. Which of the Doctor's companions was almost eaten alive by ants?
3. Which of the Doctor's companions became the Chosen One of Aukon?
4. Why at the end of *The Hand of Fear* did the Doctor leave Sarah Jane?
5. Which of the Doctor's companions first met at the Inferno Disco in Covent Garden in 1966?
6. In which century was Vicki born?
7. Which of the Doctor's friends tried to kill him in *Terror of the Autons*? Why?
8. Which member of the TARDIS crew was used as a medium by the Xeraphin to enlist the Doctor's help?
9. Why was K9 unable to take part in the Doctor and Romana's adventure on Argolis?
10. To whom did Vicki entrust the wounded Steven during the Sack of Troy?
11. Edward Waterfield entrusted the safety of his daughter Victoria to the Doctor. Nevertheless, the Time Lord did take the girl to some dangerous places. Where did Victoria travel to in her first trip in the TARDIS?
12. Which of the Doctor's companions was affectionately known by one of her fellow passengers as 'Duchess'?
13. Ian Chesterton found himself trapped in some strange

places during his time with the Doctor. In which adventure was he trapped inside a matchbox?

14. Which of the Doctor's companions won a star for mathematical excellence?
15. In which adventure did Susan become Barbara's handmaiden?
16. Name all the Doctor's companions who appeared in *The Five Doctors*. Which of these companions also helped him on Gallifrey?
17. In which adventures were Leela and Sarah Jane temporarily blinded?
18. Name Leela's father. How did he die?
19. What bargain was struck between the Black Guardian and Turlough?
20. Which of the Doctor's companions was a skilled bio-engineer?

The Adventures of the Fourth Doctor/1

1. On which planet visited by the Doctor did the two warring races live in domed cities?
2. Who was the Cailleach?
3. Which alien race can travel along any wavelength, including thought waves?
4. How was Eldrad finally destroyed on Kastria?
5. On which planet were the radiation levels so high that the Doctor and Romana had to take anti-radiation capsules?
6. What was the Nova Device?
7. Who took over the running of the Leisure Hive after the death of Morix?
8. By what name was the special guard of the Collector on Pluto known?
9. How did the Doctor persuade Sutekh to allow him, rather than Marcus Scarman, to take the TARDIS to the Pyramids of Mars?
10. What was Sutekh's gift to all humanity?
11. Name the Deciders at the time of the Doctor's visit to Alzarius.

12. Both the second and the third Doctor have fought the Minotaur. Which similar monster was encountered by the fourth Doctor and Romana?
13. Professor Marius, under the Doctor's instruction, made clone copies of the Time Lord and Leela. How did he then transfer the clones into the Doctor's body?
14. Which member of the Galsec team betrayed his comrades to Styre the Sontaran?
15. Which of the Doctor's companions was sentenced to a public steaming?
16. Why did the Doctor attempt to break into the Relic Cabinet containing the Crown Jewels of Ribos?
17. Who gave the Universe a simple choice between total annihilation and a continued existence under his guidance?
18. Name two of the scientific staff at the Research Centre near Fetch Wood.
19. How was the Elixir of Life formed on Karn?
20. What is a Laserson Probe? To what use was it put when the TARDIS landed on board the Sandminer?

The Key to Time/1

1. Why was the Key to Time split into six segments?
2. What formed the centre of the Key to Time?
3. On which planet did the Doctor and Romana find the first segment of the Key to Time?
4. Who did Garron believe the Doctor and Romana to be?
5. Whose help did the Graf Vynda Ka enlist to track down the Doctor?
6. The Pirate Captain's attention was drawn to Earth because of its abundant quantities of the mineral PJX18. What was PJX18 and why did the Pirate Captain need it?
7. What were the Pirate Captain's 'trophies'?
8. The Pirate Captain appeared to be the ruler of Zanak. Who was his and the planet's true ruler?
9. What lay three miles below the surface of Zanak?
10. Who was Mr Fibuli?

11. To which planet were the Megara travelling? Why?
12. How were Vivien Fay's wand and the Doctor's hyper-space projector powered?
13. Of what crimes was Cessair guilty?
14. The Megara refused to probe Cessair's mind to discover her true identity. How did the Doctor persuade them to do so?
15. What was the corresponding location in real space of the prison ship in hyper-space which carried the Megara?

The Adventures of the Fifth Doctor/1

1. After leaving the Pharos Project on Earth, why did Tegan and Nyssa take the fifth Doctor to the Zero Room?
2. Who created Castrovalva?
3. The TARDIS landed on a paradise planet known as planet S14. By which other name did the crew know the planet?
4. What is the symbol of the Mara?
5. What is a Monopticon?
6. Who was Dojjen?
7. The Terileptils who came to Earth were escaped convicts. From which prison planet had they escaped?
8. How was the Mara originally brought into being?
9. What is the Death Zone on Gallifrey?
10. Why were the Urbankans forced to leave their home planet?
11. What were the Plasmatons?
12. How did Mawdryn and his company hope to achieve eternal life for themselves? What went disastrously wrong with the experiment?
13. Who was Talor? Who killed him?
14. Who were the Vanir? Name their leader when the Doctor and his friends first met them. Who succeeded him?
15. Who was Shardovan?
16. Where on Gallifrey was Rassilon's Tomb located?
17. Where did the TARDIS materialise in the year 2526?

18. What is the function of the Windchimes on Deva Loka?
19. Where was the Doctor intending to take Nyssa and Tegan when the TARDIS materialised in mid-air above Heathrow?
20. What is the Flesh Time?

The Master/1

1. How did the Master hope to alter the course of English history?
2. How many bodies has the Master had?
3. Name the Chinese Security Officer of the World Peace Conference who was the puppet of the Master.
4. During his first encounter with the Master on Earth the Doctor came into possession of the dematerialisation circuit of the Master's TARDIS. Why was the Doctor unable to use this circuit to replace his damaged one?
5. How did the Master learn of the Doctor and Jo's presence in the year 2540?
6. The Master has often assumed disguises to assist him in his evil deeds. What aliases did he assume in (a) *Frontier in Space*; (b) *Castrovalva*; (c) *Colony in Space*; (d) *The King's Demons*?
7. In which adventure was the Master finally arrested?
8. Where on Earth was he imprisoned? In which story did he escape from his prison?
9. Why did the Master need the Doctor's TARDIS on prehistoric Earth?
10. What conclusive proof did the Doctor find to show that the Master had escaped from Traken?
11. Upon discovering that the Master had infiltrated his TARDIS after escaping from Traken, what bizarre scheme did the Doctor hit upon to flush the evil Time Lord out?
12. How did the Master attempt to kill the Doctor on Logopolis?
13. The Doctor managed to possess the Master's demateri-alisation circuit in *Terror of the Autons*, thereby

23

grounding his enemy's TARDIS. How and when did the Master retrieve the circuit?

14. How did the Master come to learn of the location of the Doomsday Weapon and the existence of the Sea Devils?
15. To which planet did the fifth Doctor banish the Master? How did he do this?

The Time Lords/1

1. Co-ordinator Engin described Earth as an 'interesting little planet', which had been visited by several graduates of the Time Lord Academy. Name three of them.
2. Name three chapters of Time Lords.
3. What form did Omega's TARDIS take when it landed in Amsterdam?
4. On his first return trip to Gallifrey after his trial, before which important event did the Doctor arrive?
5. Name the two Time Lords who entered into mental battle inside the Matrix.
6. Why did the Time Lords send the first Doctor to confront his two future selves in *The Three Doctors*?
7. How did the Doctor learn of the assassination of the President of the Time Lords in *The Deadly Assassin*?
8. By what right did the Doctor claim the Presidency of the Time Lords when he returned to Gallifrey at the time of the Vardan/Sontaran invasion of his home planet?
9. Capital punishment has long since been abolished on Gallifrey and there has only been one instance in history in which a Time Lord has been terminated by his fellows. Who was the Time Lord who was condemned to death?
10. Where on Gallifrey did K'anpo live?
11. How did Omega generate the power needed for his transfer from the Universe of anti-matter to our Universe?
12. Who tried to turn themselves into Time Lords?
13. Name the Time Lord in charge of security of the Citadel on Gallifrey.
14. How was the Doctor's TARDIS grounded on Gallifrey

during the time of Omega's second attempt to enter the Universe of matter?

15. Who was the misguided Time Lord who betrayed his people in an attempt to bring Omega into the world of matter?

The Adventures of the First Doctor/2

1. Name the long-lost sister planet of Earth. What was its ultimate fate?
2. Who was Vasor?
3. How did the Doctor, convinced that Ian and Barbara were plotting against him, plan to deal with them in *The Brink of Disaster*?
4. The atmosphere of Vortis is quite thin compared to Earth's. How did the Doctor and Ian compensate for this when they landed on the Web Planet?
5. Who was Wulnoth?
6. How did the Doctor, Steven and Sara travel from Earth to Mira in the 41st century?
7. Who were the Monoids?
8. Name the leader of the Elders and the leader of the Savages encountered by the Doctor, Steven and Dodo.
9. Name two of the Aridians encountered by the TARDIS crew.
10. Where did the Doctor believe the TARDIS to have landed when the Ship materialised at the Festival of Ghana?
11. The main obstacle preventing the Xerons from staging a successful resistance to the Moroks was their lack of weapons. How did they finally obtain arms?
12. How was the crew cut off from the TARDIS when they materialised in the London of 2164?
13. What was the Roof of the World?
14. Landing on the Earth of the 1960s the Doctor and his friends found themselves in a gully between two cliff faces. Where had they landed?
15. What was the Sand Beast? Who killed it?
16. How did the Voord survive the acid sea which

surrounded Arbitan's island on Marinus?

17. Which member of Captain Maitland's crew became insane?
18. Name the leader of Expedition Ten-Zero Alpha to Kembel.
19. After the massacre at the plateau where did Barbara and her Menoptera friends find refuge?
20. Leaving 17th-century Cornwall the Doctor announced to Polly and Ben that the TARDIS had brought them to the 'coldest place on Earth'. Where had they landed?

Adventures in History/2

1. What was the Great Horse of Asia?
2. Which intelligent creatures ruled the Earth before Man?
3. Which band of outlaws constantly threatened the security of Edward of Wessex in the 12th century?
4. Where did Professor Hayter believe himself to be when he was thrown back 140 million years in time?
5. How did the Doctor and Steven hope to escape from Odysseus in *The Myth Makers*?
6. Who were the Brethren of Demnos?
7. The Doctor, Ben and Polly met a motley band of rogues when the TARDIS materialised on the Cornish coast in the 17th century. Who was (a) Cherub; (b) Holy Joe Longford; (c) Jacob Kewper?
8. In which adventure did the Doctor escape from gaol and disguise himself as a kitchen wench?
9. What was the Tong of the Black Scorpion?
10. On the shores of which river did George Cranleigh find the Black Orchid?
11. Richard Mace saw a comet in the sky and took it to be a portent of plague. What was it in reality?
12. Landing in 13th-century England, the Doctor, Tegan and Turlough became the guests of which lord and lady?
13. Who guarded the Crystal of Kronos in ancient Atlantis?
14. What was the ruse whereby the Doctor and Ian escaped from the Earl of Leicester and his men?

15. Who helped the ancient Britons to build Stonehenge?
16. Why did Ike, Billy and Phineas Clanton plan to kill Doc Holliday?
17. Robespierre's deputy, Paul Barrass, arranged to meet his fellow conspirator in The Sinking Ship, an inn to the north of Paris. Who was his fellow plotter?
18. How did the Doctor inadvertently become engaged to the Aztec lady Cameca?
19. Who were Sevcheria and Didius?
20. Put the following adventures in their chronological order in the history of Earth: *The King's Demons*; *The Tribe of Gum*; *The Massacre*; *The Highlanders*; *Black Orchid*; *The Crusaders*.

The Adventures of the Second Doctor/2

1. Who was the Earthman who served the Master Brain in the Land of Fiction?
2. Who were the Masters of the Ten Galaxies?
3. Who was Medok?
4. Name the T-Mat supremo in the 21st century.
5. Who are the Quarks?
6. Who promised to lift Atlantis out of the sea? How did he propose to do this?
7. Why was it vitally important for the personnel of the Britannicus Ice Base to discover the propulsion system of the Ice Warriors's ship?
8. What alien creatures attacked Space Station W3 LX88J?
9. Name the traveller from Nottingham whom the second Doctor and his friends encountered.
10. Why did the War Lord and his people intend to employ Earthmen in their army to conquer the galaxy?
11. In *Fury From The Deep* the second Doctor flew a helicopter. How did he say he had learnt to fly such a machine?
12. What nationality was Salamander?
13. Arriving in Inverness in search of the Doctor, Ben,

Jamie and his laird, what disguises did Polly and Kirsty assume?

14. How did Selris hope to lure the Krotons out of their Dynotrope?

15. In which adventure did the TARDIS become invisible?

16. Who were Wahed, Etnin and Tolata?

17. At the beginning of *The Wheel in Space*, it was necessary for the Doctor to remove the TARDIS's Time Vector Generator, thereby separating the time machine's interior and exterior dimensions and changing the TARDIS into an ordinary police box. Why was it necessary to do this?

18. Who betrayed Salamander and presented Giles Kent with damning evidence of the would-be dictator's evil deeds?

19. How did the Doctor and his friends travel from Victorian England to Skaro?

20. Why were Astrid Ferrier and Giles Kent so interested in the Doctor when the TARDIS materialised in Australia?

Companions of the Doctor/2

1. Name all the Doctor's companions who were not born on Earth.

2. From what fate did the Doctor save K9 in *The Armageddon Factor*?

3. Which member of the TARDIS crew contracted Lazars' disease?

4. How did Turlough contact the Black Guardian?

5. Name the first mate of Captain Striker who was so fascinated with Tegan.

6. Which of the Doctor's companions worked for a while in the Bureau of Ancient Records on Gallifrey?

7. After his adventure in Troy, Steven fell ill with blood poisoning brought about from an injury he had sustained. Who cured him?

8. What ruse did Jamie use to commend himself to Salamander?

9. Who was the Princess of TARDIS?
10. Where did Ben and Polly's first visit in the TARDIS take them to?
11. How did Omega learn of Tegan's acquaintance with the Doctor?
12. Why did Tegan rejoin the TARDIS crew?
13. Why was Rorvik particularly interested in Romana?
14. Why did Nyssa leave the Doctor, Tegan and Turlough?
15. Name the Doctor's companions who have been members of the Navy.
16. Which of the Doctor's companions were taken over by WOTAN?
17. Realising that Turlough would never kill the Doctor, what supreme punishment did the Black Guardian mete out to the boy?
18. Why was Jamie hospitalised when the TARDIS crew landed on the moon?
19. Tegan entered the TARDIS when the car in which she was travelling to start her new job as a stewardess blew a tyre. Her very first job as a stewardess was not quite in the situation she might have imagined. What was it?
20. Which of the Doctor's companions were trapped inside the TARDIS when it was surrounded by Cybermen on Gallifrey?

The Cybermen/1

1. Name the home planet of the Cybermen.
2. How was it destroyed?
3. Why did the Cybermen attempt to destroy Earth in the 26th century?
4. Who was General Cutler?
5. Name the captain of the Earth freighter which was taken over by the Cybermen.
6. How did Vorus plan to destroy the Cybermen?
7. Sarah Jane Smith was infected by a Cybermat on Nerva. How was she cured?
8. Who guarded the Cybermen's bomb on the Earth of the 26th century?

9. What was the mission of the *Zeus Five* spacecraft?
10. How many Cyberships came to Earth in *The Tenth Planet?*
11. Which planet played a crucial role in the defeat of the Cybermen in the Great Cyberwar?
12. How did the Commanding Officer of the Snowcap Tracking Base propose to destroy the planet of the Cybermen?
13. What manner of machine succeeded in almost totally destroying a group of Cybermen on Gallifrey?
14. What had brought Professor Kyle's party to the caves in which the Cybermen's deadly bomb was hidden?
15. How did Tobias Vaughn communicate with his Cybermen allies in space?
16. Name the Frenchman who was second-in-command at the Moon Base.
17. Why did the disease introduced by the Cybermen to the Moon Base only affect certain members of the Base's personnel?
18. Ever wary of his allies, Tobias Vaughn had devised a means by which he could destroy the Cybermen. What was it?
19. Why did the Cybermen use a bomb in their attempt to destroy Earth in the 26th century rather than a missile?
20. What plan did they adopt when the Doctor successfully defused their bomb?

The Adventures of the Third Doctor/2

1. Who tamed the sacred beast of Peladon?
2. Why did Mr and Mrs Jones go on an expedition up the Amazon?
3. Name all the members of the expedition to Exxilon.
4. What brought the Doctor to the Research Institute in *The Time Warrior?*
5. Name the hermaphrodite hexapod encountered by the Doctor.
6. How did the Doctor and Jo travel from Skybase One down to the surface of Solos?

7. The Keller Machine was capable of killing people by instilling in their minds the thing they were most afraid of. Which natural element was the third Doctor especially afraid of?
8. Name Professor Keller's assistant in England.
9. When the guerillas from the 22nd century travelled back to the 20th century they attempted to kill the Doctor. Why?
10. What do the initials IMC stand for? Why did the IMC come to the planet of the Doomsday Weapon?
11. Name the head of IMC's operations on that planet.
12. After the Doctor defeated Grun in the Pit of Combat on Peladon, who attempted to kill the Time Lord? Who saved him?
13. How did the third Doctor and his Thal allies escape from the Dalek city on Spiridon?
14. Who was Shirna?
15. Name the children of Sabor and Neska.
16. From what did Axos draw power to generate enough energy to make a time jump?
17. Who was Doctor Quinn?
18. Name the head of the Coven at Devil's End.
19. Who was the military aide of the President of Earth in the year 2540?
20. What special properties did the blue crystal which the Doctor took from Metebelis 3 have?

The Daleks and the Thals/2

1. Who led the Daleks during their first invasion of Earth in the 22nd century?
2. Why did the Daleks send Susan to collect the anti-radiation drugs left for the TARDIS crew by Alydon?
3. Why were the Daleks so interested in these drugs?
4. Davros, the creator of the Daleks, could only travel around in a wheelchair and all of his life-functions were artificially maintained. What had crippled him so?
5. Who saved the Doctor and his friends from the Pursuer Daleks in *The Chase* and then imprisoned them in a zoo?

6. What was the Day of Armageddon?
7. The Daleks' exterminator guns were rendered useless on Exxilon. How then did they arm themselves?
8. How did the Thals originally plan to destroy the Dalek City on Spiridon?
9. Which Thal became particularly fond of Barbara on Skaro?
10. How did the Thals hope finally to defeat the Kaleds and end their ages-long war?
11. Who saved the Doctor and Jo from the Dalek headquarters on Earth? Why?
12. Where did the Daleks on Skaro, who were encountered by the first Doctor and his friends, get their water from?
13. What was the cause of the death of the Daleks in Section Three of their city on Ckaro at the time of the first Doctor's visit there?
14. Who were Hyksos and Khephren?
15. How did Susan and David Campbell temporarily immobilise the Daleks in 2164?
16. How did Davros plan to destroy the Movellan spaceship before it could leave Skaro?
17. After their departure from Exxilon, how did the Daleks intend to destroy all life on the planet?
18. The Daleks came to Spiridon to make use of the planet's icecanos. Why did the Thals think the Daleks had come to the planet?
19. Why did the Daleks invade Earth in (a) *The Dalek Invasion of Earth*; (b) *Day of the Daleks*?
20. Tried and tested solutions are often the best. What identical ruse did the first Doctor and his friends use to escape from the Dalek City on Skaro, and the third Doctor and his friends use to enter the Dalek City on Spiridon?

The Adventures of the Fourth Doctor/2

1. What is the TARDIS cloister bell? In which adventure was it first used?
2. Who was Organon?
3. Which alien species decided to colonise Earth after the levels of radioactivity on their own planet became intolerably high?
4. Where is the planet Diplos?
5. What did the Marshmen on Alzarius plan to use as a battering ram against the Starliner?
6. Jackson and his colleagues left their home world some 100,000 years before the Doctor and Leela met them. How had they survived for such a great period of time?
7. How did Eldrad gain the power to regenerate?
8. What was the Mordee Expedition?
9. Exactly when and where on Earth did the Jagaroth spaceship carrying the last of that race land?
10. How did the Doctor rekindle the dying Sacred Flame on Karn?
11. Who was Sir Colin Thackerey?
12. Who was Professor Theodore Kerensky? How did he die?
13. What was the fate of those peasant youths selected by Aukon?
14. How did the Doctor save himself and the TARDIS from being struck by the planetoid in *The Horns of Nimon*?
15. Name the very mad scientist who was brought up by robots until he believed himself to be one and organised their rebellion.
16. Who was Ravon?
17. Name three of the Consuls of Traken.
18. What does the word 'Melkur' mean?
19. Who pursued the Doctor and his friends through the corridors of the TARDIS?
20. What is a Janis Thorn?

1. Who are the Eternals?
2. Who are the Ephemerals?
3. What is Terminus?
4. Who are the Snakedancers?
5. Why were the Xeraphin forced to leave their home world and seek a new home on prehistoric Earth?
6. What is Event One?
7. The first Doctor, wary of changing the course of history, declined saving Anne Chaplette from almost certain death in the Massacre of St Bartholomew's Eve. Who else would the Doctor not save by travelling back in time?
8. Name the leaders of (a) the Mayans; (b) the Aborigines; (c) the Chinese on board Monarch's ship.
9. In which constellation was Castrovalva?
10. Who became the Doctor's squire when the TARDIS materialised in England in 1215?
11. After the death of Panna, into which member of the Kinda did all her knowledge pass?
12. What is the Box of Jana?
13. How did the Doctor save the TARDIS from destruction in Event One?
14. Name all the members of the Dome on Deva Loka.
15. Upon learning of its existence, where did Captain Striker and his officers hide the TARDIS?
16. Who did Tegan and Nyssa initially think Mawdryn to be?
17. Who was Kamilion?
18. Name the Director on Manussa during the Doctor's visit to that planet. Who was his predecessor?
19. By what name did the Kinda know the people of the Dome?
20. Who was Kalid?

1. What is a Metamorphic Symbiosis Generator? Who stole one from Gallifrey?
2. Name the Lord President and the Chancellor of the Time Lords during the time of Omega's second attempt to enter the Universe of matter.
3. How long can a Time Lord stay alive in the sub-zero emptiness of space?
4. Which of the following Time Lords is the odd one out? Why? (a) Borusa; (b) the Doctor; (c) Zorac.
5. Why did Chancellor Goth ally himself with the Master on Gallifrey?
6. Name three instances when the Doctor's TARDIS has been operated by remote control by the Time Lords.
7. Why did Morbius and his followers come to Karn?
8. Brought to Gallifrey to face trial, how did the War Lord attempt to escape?
9. All but one member of the High Council of Time Lords agreed to the Doctor's termination on Gallifrey. Which one?
10. What was the main line of defence used by the second Doctor in his trial on Gallifrey?
11. The Meddling Monk came up with quite an intriguing scheme to make a fortune. What was it?
12. What do the Time Lords Goth, Borusa and the Doctor all have in common?
13. Which Doctor fought the dark side of Omega's mind?
14. Who killed the President of the Time Lords in *The Deadly Assassin*? Who was at first thought to have done so?
15. Who succeeded to the Presidency of the Time Lords after the disgrace of Borusa?

1. What was the Khazenome?
2. Where was the Snowcap Tracking Station located?
3. The Sontarans are an asexual clone species capable of multiplying at the rate of several thousands per minute. Which other race of clones were encountered by the Doctor, Steven and Vicki?
4. Which race held the Doctor in great esteem, having followed his journies through time and space?
5. Who was Professor Krimpton?
6. Faced with a power loss on Exxilon, the third Doctor opened the TARDIS doors with an old-fashioned hand crank. When the Animus on Vortis had drained the TARDIS of much of its power, how did the first Doctor open the doors of the Ship?
7. The Aridians shared their planet with the deadly Mire Beasts. How did they attempt to destroy their enemies who multiplied at an alarming rate?
8. Who were Doctor Caligari, Dodo Dupont and Steven Regret?
9. What was the Cave of Five Hundred Eyes?
10. Who attempted to attack Ian with a pair of scissors?
11. Who were Dargenson and Rouvray?
12. Leela initially believed the Doctor to be a great magician and the TARDIS some sort of deity. Who believed the Doctor to be a god who would take her to the Place of Perfection?
13. Who were Sergeant Rugg and Mrs Wiggs?
14. Name the Head of Security and Mavic Chen's deputy on the Earth of the 41st century.
15. Who was Tor in (a) *The Space Museum*; (b) *The Savages*?
16. In which city in North England did the Doctor, Steven and Sara spend an eventful Christmas?
17. How and where did Bennett meet his death on Dido?
18. Where is the planet Quinnis?
19. How did the Rills communicate with the Doctor and Vicki?
20. Who activated the Time Destructor which resulted in

the devastation of Kembel and the death of Sara Kingdom?

Adventures in History/3

1. Arriving at various periods in the history of our planet, the Doctor often finds himself caught up in the tide of events and forced to act. How did he convince Sarah Jane that they had to defeat Sutekh in 1911 rather than simply return to present-day Earth?
2. Name the daughter of Jamie's clan laird who helped the TARDIS crew in 18th-century Scotland.
3. What gift did the Emperor Nero present to Barbara? What important role did it play in the schoolteacher's next adventure?
4. Why did Tavannes order the murder of the Abbot of Amboise?
5. Who was Ping-Cho?
6. What was the Masque of Mandragora?
7. Name the young Venetian who left his home town with his father and uncle in 1271 and became a respected friend of mighty Kublai Khan.
8. Catherine de' Medici ordered the Massacre of St Bartholomew's Eve in which thousands of Huguenots were murdered by the Catholic mob. One particular Huguenot however was spared. Who was he, and why did the Queen Mother reluctantly agree to spare him?
9. Who was Ann Talbot?
10. Richard Mace's necklace was not of this Earth. What was it?
11. Why, when the TARDIS materialised in England on 4, March 1215, was the Doctor so suspicious of the identity of King John?
12. Why was Tegana travelling to Shang-Tu in 1289?
13. Which member of the tribe of Gum was initially accused of the murder of Old Mother? How did the Doctor expose the real murderer?
14. Who killed Achilles the Greek?
15. Who was Josiah Blake?

16. What destroyed the dinosaurs?
17. Why did King Richard the Lionheart make Ian Chesterton a knight?
18. Who were the King's Demons?
19. Who killed Irongron?
20. Which of these historical characters has the Doctor never met? (a) Leonardo da Vinci; (b) Catherine di' Medici; (c) Nero; (d) Richard the Lionheart; (e) Pyrrho.

The Adventures of the Second Doctor/3

1. Faced with the failure of all his plans for world domination, Salamander made one last attempt to escape justice. What was it?
2. Name four members of the crew of the Wheel in Space.
3. Which members of the TARDIS crew were sent to work in the gas pits of the colony threatened by the Macra?
4. Who was Megan Jones?
5. Where did the Doctor gain his medical degree?
6. Who was the Karkus?
7. Name the Controller of the Central European Zone and his deputy in *Enemy of the World*.
8. Twenty years before the TARDIS crew met him, Professor Zaroff disappeared from public life. Both the East and the West blamed each other for his disappearance and suggested that the other power bloc had kidnapped him. What had happened to him?
9. Who captured a Yeti for the Doctor in Tibet?
10. Name the leader of the Dulcians and the father of Cully.
11. Name the General who had been pursuing Caven and his pirates for some time before the Doctor, Jamie and Zoe became involved with the space pirates.
12. How did Caven ensure the continued co-operation of Madeleine Issigri?
13. How was the Great Intelligence finally defeated in Tibet?
14. Captured by the British soldiers of the First World War, the Doctor, Jamie and Zoe were found guilty of being spies. What sentence was passed on each of them?

15. Name the Chief of Police in the colony threatened by the Macra.
16. What was the Power of the Daleks?
17. How were the Doctor, Jamie and Zoe separated from the TARDIS when it landed on Space Beacon Alpha Four?
18. What was the fate of those Gond scholars who entered the Dynotrope?
19. Name three of the monks at the monastery of Det-sen.
20. What is argonite?

UNIT

1. What is the Brigadier's personal call sign?
2. Why did Tyler contact UNIT in *The Three Doctors*?
3. Name the Brigadier's deputy during the first Nestene invasion of Earth.
4. UNIT was called in to investigate power losses from the cyclotron at Wenley Moor research station. What was causing these power losses?
5. Name the Doctor's first assistant at UNIT.
6. Why had a division of UNIT been sent to Scotland in *Terror of the Zygons*?
7. Who was Bill Filer? Why did he involve himself in the affairs of UNIT?
8. Who was General Scobie?
9. UNIT infiltrated the Think Tank with a secret agent. Who was he, and what identity did he assume?
10. How did UNIT break through the heat barrier which surrounded Devil's End?
11. Faced with facts which seem to contradict most of the known laws of science, the Brigadier has often tried to provide rational explanations for the strange events which have befallen him. Transported to Omega's world, for instance, he believed that the Doctor had somehow taken him to Cromer! How did he account for the second Doctor's sudden reappearance in the same adventure?
12. Why did Mike Yates attend K'anpo's meditation centre?
13. Upon his second meeting with the Doctor, the Brigadier

was concerned about several UFO sightings in south-east England. What evil did these UFOs bring to Earth?

14. During the attack of the Krynoid, the Brigadier was away in Geneva. Who deputised for him?

15. Which member of UNIT infiltrated Global Chemicals by posing as a ministry official?

16. Who was first offered the job of UNIT's scientific advisor?

17. What did RSM Benton and Harry Sullivan do after they left UNIT?

18. What caused the Brigadier's amnesia and mental breakdown in 1977?

19. Upon landing in Terminal One at Heathrow, the Doctor was faced with awkward questions about the presence of a certain blue police box. How did he extricate himself from this embarrassing situation and at the same time get involved in the mystery of a missing Concorde?

20. What did the Brigadier do after he retired from ENIT?

General/2

1. With the exception of his third incarnation, each Doctor and his friends have at one time or another met his double. Name all these instances.

2. What is the better known name of the planet listed in the Movellan star catalogue as D Five Gamma Z Alpha?

3. Which was the computer who (a) thought it was a god; (b) tried to control the world from the Post Office tower; (c) was built by a Time Lord and almost destroyed a planet?

4. Who was Rossini in (a) *Terror of the Autons*; (b) *The Masque of Mandragora*?

5. Which of these alien species is the odd one out? Why? (a) Visians; (b) Spiridons; (c) Sontarans; (d) Refusians.

6. Which two brothers, each of whom became King, have been met by the Doctor – or so it seemed?

7. Who were (a) the Mutts; (b) the Mutos?

8. What is Lazars' Disease?

9. The Doctor's sonic screwdriver made its first appearance

in *Fury from the Deep*. In which adventure was it finally destroyed?

10. In which adventure did Romana's sonic screwdriver make its one and only appearance?
11. What is a Cyborg?
12. Name the handmaiden of (a) Queen Galleia of Atlantis; (b) the Empress Poppea; (c) Cassandra.
13. What wording appears on the TARDIS doors?
14. Which of the following planets is the odd one out? Why? (a) Dido; (b) Leela's homeworld; (c) Dulkis; (d) Mars; (e) Skaro.
15. In *The Three Doctors* and *The Five Doctors* the first law of time was violated when the Doctor crossed his own timestream and met his other selves. Which of the Doctor's friends has also crossed his own time stream?

The Adventures of the Third Doctor/3

1. What was the IRIS Machine? In which adventure was it used?
2. Who was Vega Nexos?
3. Name the Captain of the Naval Base which was threatened by the Sea Devils.
4. Who was the advance guard of the first Nestene invasion of Earth? Who created him?
5. Who was Bok?
6. The TOMTIT Machine was capable, among other things, of altering the flow of time. Whom did it transform into a baby and whom into a decrepit old man?
7. Who were the Functionaries?
8. The three guerillas who travelled through time in an attempt to prevent the Third World War were Anat, Boaz and Shura. Who was the leader of the expedition?
9. Name three members of the Colony in Space.
10. Where exactly in South England did Axos land? Why?
11. Who was Amazonia?
12. On what did the Eight Legs of Metebelis 3 feed?
13. Who was the leader of the opposition on Earth in 2540?

What policy did he advocate in the conflict between Earth and Draconia?

14. Who was Eckersley?
15. The Doctor was instrumental in persuading the Time Lords to ban the use of Miniscopes. What is a Miniscope?
16. What was the Time Scoop?
17. Who was the great wizard Quiquaequod?
18. Name the planet on which the Doomsday Weapon was located.
19. When the Doctor first visited Peladon the posts of Chancellor and High Priest were two separate offices, held respectively by Torbis and Hepesh. Fifty years later, the two posts had been merged into one. Who held the office of Chancellor and High Priest of Peladon under the reign of Queen Thalira?
20. How did the Doctor finally defeat Axos?

The Adventures of the Fourth Doctor/3

1. Why was Logopolis absolutely crucial to the survival of the Universe?
2. What was the standard unit of currency on Pluto during the Company's control of that planet?
3. Who were Nesbin and Presta?
4. A Sevateem ritual to ward off evil was a symbolic touching of the throat, shoulder and hip. What were the origins of this ritual?
5. How was the Fendahl on Earth destroyed? How did the Doctor destroy the Fendahl skull?
6. Who were the Trogs?
7. Why could the people of the Starliner never return to Terradon?
8. What did the Doctor, Romana and Duggan find in a hidden chamber in the cellar of the house of Count Scarlioni?
9. The planet Pluto was thought to be the outermost planet of Earth's solar system before the discovery of which celestial body?

10. The Doctor was present with the Philippino army for the battle of which Icelandic city in the 51st century?
11. What four types of robot were to be found on board the Sandminer?
12. How were the Wirrn finally defeated?
13. How did the Watcher protect Adric and Nyssa from the growing entropy field in *Logopolis*?
14. What deal had Lord Palmerdale and Colonel Skinsdale come to before they became shipwrecked at Fang Rock?
15. Why were Zadek and Farrah so interested in the Doctor on Tara?
16. How did the Company ensure full co-operation with their schemes on Pluto?
17. Why did the Kraals need the androids to help them in their invasion of Earth? How were the androids sent to Earth?
18. The Doctor and Adric's visit to Traken probably saw the greatest number of Keepers ever in such a short time. Name all the Keepers in this period.
19. Which creature lived off death itself?
20. The Doctor has repeatedly stated that it is impossible to alter the past. Nevertheless he did try to do so once. When?

The Daleks and the Thals/3

1. The Daleks and the Thals are not the only examples of Skaroine life to have been encountered by the Doctor and his friends. Name two others.
2. When he and Susan were captured in the Dalek City on Skaro how did the Doctor attempt to strike a bargain with the Daleks?
3. To whom did the Daleks promise to give the secret of turning lead into gold?
4. What fate befell Sarah Jane when she was taken prisoner by the Thals on Skaro?
5. The Daleks' research into invisibility on Spiridon had one unfortunate effect for them. What was it?
6. What ultimatum did Mogren and his colleagues present to Davros?

7. How did the first Doctor learn of the Daleks' Master Plan in the 41st century?

8. On whom did the Daleks test the core of their Time Destructor? What happened to him when the Daleks discovered the core to be a fake?

9. Where in London was the Daleks' saucer parked during their first invasion of Earth in the 22nd century?

10. How did the first Doctor and his friends defeat the Daleks who had invaded Earth in the 22nd century?

11. The Doctor found a highly appropriate way to destroy the tape on which was recorded a catalogue of future Dalek defeats. What was it?

12. The Spar 7-40 was the spacecraft of which member of the Daleks' Grand Alliance?

13. How did Davros betray his own people to the Thals? Why did he do this?

14. What plan did the Central Committee of Earth guerillas of the 22nd century devise to utterly defeat the Daleks?

15. Name the leader of the rebels on the Vulcan colony threatened by the Daleks.

16. How did the Daleks attempt to deal with all opposition to them on Spiridon? How was this plan thwarted?

17. Discovering that they had become dependent on the radiation which soaked Skaro, the Daleks decided to explode a second neutron bomb which would also have the added advantage of exterminating the Thals. However when it was decided that the twenty-three days to construct such a bomb was too long, what alternative plan did they adopt?

18. How were the Daleks on Kembel finally defeated?

19. Although the Daleks have proved to be the Doctor's most persistent enemies, several of the Time Lord's companions have never met them. Which of the following have never encountered the monsters from Skaro? Jamie; Zoe; Jo; Katarina; Steven; Polly; Harry.

20. In which adventure did the Doctor believe he had witnessed the final end of the Daleks?

1. What is Enlightenment?
2. What lies at the centre of the Universe?
3. Who were Anithon and Zarak?
4. What method of propulsion was used by the ships of the Eternals?
5. Who defeated the Mara for the first time on Manussa?
6. Who was the Garm?
7. What are Recreationals?
8. One of Terminus's fuel tanks overloaded and was jettisoned millenia ago. When the Doctor arrived on Terminus he managed to prevent the second fuel tank from exploding. What would have been the consequences if he had failed?
9. What was the Ergon?
10. What was the source of the Portreeve's great wisdom?
11. How did the Mara bring itself home to Manussa?
12. Following the flight path of Speedbird Concorde 192 where did the second Concorde arrive? Where did the crew think they had landed until the Doctor dispelled the illusion?
13. What were the marker buoys used by the Eternals?
14. What was the cause of the energy drain which the TARDIS experienced after leaving Terminus?
15. Voice is a sign of wisdom among the Kinda. How did the male Kinda communicate with each other?
16. What is a bonding? Who attempted to bond with the Doctor?
17. What was Monarch's ultimate aim?
18. How did the Company ensure the continued co-operation of the Vanir on Terminus? How was the Company's hold on the Vanir finally broken?
19. What was the prize sought by Captains Striker and Wrack?
20. How did Captain Wrack destroy her rivals?

1. Whom did the Doctor describe as his second best friend?
2. How did Nyssa destroy the Terileptil android which boarded the TARDIS?
3. Which of the Doctor's companions helped the Mara to manifest itself on Deva Loka and Manussa?
4. What plan did Adric have for destroying Melkur? What dire consequensces would this action have had?
5. Who was the Phantom Piper of the McCrimmon clan?
6. Which of the Doctor's companions have been tele-pathic?
7. Who sent Romana to help the Doctor in the quest for the Key to Time? Who did Romana believe had sent her?
8. How did Katarina die?
9. Why did Nyssa not take part in the adventure on Deva Loka?
10. Which member of the TARDIS crew died in an attempt to save Earth?
11. On what day did Tegan first enter the TARDIS?
12. Which member of the TARDIS crew was held hostage by the Ice Warriors on Earth during its second Ice Age?
13. Of all the monsters she encountered during her travels, and with the possible exception of the giant maggots, which one did Jo fear the most?
14. Which of the Doctor's companions was asked to marry (a) a Duke; (b) a King; (c) a sacrificial victim?
15. Name the two instances when Turlough attempted to kill the Doctor.
16. Travelling with the Doctor is not without its dangers. Several of the Time Lord's companions have been aged almost to death although only one has ever died. Which companion died of old age within sight of the TARDIS?
17. Which of the Doctor's companions did not know how many shillings there were in a pound?
18. While most of the Doctor's Earth companions have been born in the 20th century, several of the TARDIS passengers have come from the past or future of this planet. Which of his companions did the Doctor meet in: (a) 1746; (b) 1867; (c) the end of the 25th century; (d)

4000; (e) 1200 BC?

19. The Doctor tried several times to take Tegan back to Heathrow before she decided to stay on board the TARDIS for a while. In each of his attempts where did the time machine materialise?

20. How was the contract between Turlough and the Black Guardian terminated?

The Adventures of the First Doctor/4

1. The fifth Doctor has often displayed his fondness for cricket. In which adventure did the TARDIS land briefly at the Oval in the middle of a cricket match?

2. What was the Temple of Secrets?

3. What exactly was the Trilogic Game?

4. In *The Edge of Destruction*, how did the TARDIS warn its passengers that it was heading backwards to the dawn of time and certain destruction?

5. Unlike our Earth, the Gonds' planet was lit by the light of two suns. Which other planet visited by the Doctor, Ian, Barbara and Vicki was part of a binary system?

6. Who was the Knight of Jaffa?

7. What was DN6?

8. What was the Land of Fear?

9. Why did Tor destroy the Space Museum at the request of the Doctor?

10. Where were the dwellings of the savages on Jano's world?

11. Who discovered an antidote to the cold virus which Dodo had unwittingly brought on board the Space Ark?

12. How did the Sensorites communicate with each other over long distances?

13. Barbara and Hrostar joined a slave colony at the Crater of Needles on Vortis. What did their work there largely consist of?

14. Who were the gods of the Optera?

15. Name two members of the Optera race.

16. How did Arbitan ensure that the time travellers had no

choice but to embark on their quest for the Keys of Marinus?

17. Who visited, among others, the towns of Lop, Sinju and Cheng-Ting?

18. Captain Briggs was the captain who helped the fifth Doctor in his battle with the Cybermen. Who was Captain Benjamin Briggs?

19. How was Dodo hypnotised by WOTAN? How did the Doctor restore the girl to her senses?

20. Upon landing on Refusis, the Doctor found the planet to be populated by invisible beings. What had rendered the Refusians invisible?

The Adventures of the Second Doctor/4

1. How did the War Chief die?
2. Who demanded that Salamander show him the outside world above ground level?
3. What happened to him?
4. To whom did the Great Intelligence promise long life and great knowledge?
5. Upon arriving at the Britannicus Ice Base, the Doctor, Jamie and Victoria were assumed to be Scavengers and were allocated places on the next flight out to the more temperate climes of Africa. How did the Doctor win the confidence of those at the Ice Base?
6. How did the Doctor's favourite umbrella save him on the planet of the Gonds?
7. Who were the Scavengers?
8. Why had the Island of Death on Dulkis been uninhabited for 172 years, apart from the presence of a permanent survey unit?
9. Who were the 'high brains'?
10. How were the Ice Warriors encountered by the second Doctor armed?
11. Who very nearly turned the Doctor to stone?
12. Rago and Toba broke off from the main Dominator fleet to land on Dulkis. For which planet was the main fleet headed?

13. How did the security chief propose to solve the problem of the resistance fighters once and for all in *The War Games*?
14. Why did Rago and Toba choose to land on the Island of Death on Dulkis?
15. What holy relic did the Doctor return to the monastery of Det-sen three hundred years after its disappearance?
16. Who was Donald Bruce?
17. Name two of the time zones visited by any member of the TARDIS crew in *The War Games*.
18. By the 21st century rocket travel had become obsolete. What had replaced it?
19. Which planet produced the most argonite in the galaxy?
20. Who were the White Robots?

The Earth in Danger/2

1. What was the Festival of Ghana? Why had it to be closed?
2. WOTAN was destroyed by a War Machine which had been reprogrammed by the Doctor. How was the War Machine immobilised long enough to allow the Doctor to make the necessary adjustments to its circuitry?
3. Name the scientist who developed DN6 with financial backing from Forester.
4. Why was Salamander able to predict natural disasters with such great accuracy?
5. The fight against the Yeti during the Great Intelligence's second attack on Earth was organised from an underground fortress near Goodge Street tube station. What was the original purpose of the fortress?
6. Where in the London Underground was the Great Intelligence finally defeated?
7. How did Monarch intend to dispose of Earth's inhabitants?
8. What was Government Minister Walker's proposed solution to the problem of the Sea Devils? How did the Doctor finally defeat the underwater creatures?
9. Who took over the control of the Goodge Street fortress

from Captain Knight during the Yeti invasion of London?
10. How did the Kraals propose to rid Earth of its native population?
11. What caused World War Six?
12. Where on Earth was Sutekh's pyramid located?
13. What dire consequences did the Doctor foresee if Professor Fendelman's Time Scanner were to continue to be used?
14. Why was the Disintegrator Gun necessary to Hilda Winters' plan for world domination?
15. Who envisaged the world as 'a harmony of root, stem, leaf and flower'?

The Adventures of the Third Doctor/4

1. What was the purpose of the Keller Machine, as claimed by Professor Keller?
2. How did the Miniscope come to be in Vorg's possession?
3. What was the Nuthutch?
4. Azaxyr was the leader of a breakaway group of Ice Warriors who wanted to return to the glorious days of conquest and warfare. With which power were they in alliance?
5. The Time Lords sent the Doctor a box containing stone tablets which he was to take to Solos. For whom was the box intended and how did the Doctor attempt to discover what the box contained?
6. Name the head of Wenley Moor research station.
7. How did the Doctor defend himself and Jo against Bok when they were attacked by the imp in the barrow at Devil's End?
8. Distinguish between the Autons, the Replicas and the Nestenes.
9. Who assumed control of Skybase One after the death of the Marshal?
10. Exxilon is largely a bleak and barren planet except for the presence of which particular mineral?
11. The Master and the Daleks were almost successful in

creating a second war between Earth and Draconia. How had the first war between these two great powers come about?

12. Name the Ambassador of the Galactic Federation to Peladon during the Doctor and Sarah Jane's visit to that planet.

13. Who went off to find a maggot for Cliff Jones?

14. What were the three native species on Exarius?

15. How was the village of Devil's End sealed off during the manifestations of Azal the Daemon?

16. Who succeeded Ashe as leader of the colonists on Exarius?

17. Vorg discovered in his Miniscope a piece of foreign matter which was interfering with its smooth operation. What was it?

18. Name three of the species in Vorg's collection.

19. Name the scientist who tried to escape with the Doctor from the lunar penal colony in 2540.

20. King Peladon seemed to have a very special affection for the planet Earth. Why?

Adventures in History/4

1. Who caused the pyramids to be built?

2. Where was the Terileptil base in London situated?

3. Who possessed Magnus Greel's Time Cabinet in the London of the late 19th century? How had it come into his possession?

4. Who was Locusta? How did she earn the enmity of the Empress Poppea?

5. Which Trojan immediately befriended Vicki on her exit from the TARDIS despite the demands of Cassandra that she should be killed?

6. Which Moslem Emir attempted to kidnap King Richard the Lionheart? And whom did he capture?

7. Who was Captain Trask? Who killed him?

8. Who was the Firemaker?

9. Leaving Paris in 1979, the Doctor travelled backwards in time to meet a certain Renaissance Italian. Name him.

10. What disguise did Vicki assume when the TARDIS materialised in 12th-century Palestine?
11. Who killed the Clanton brothers at the Shootout at the OK Coral?
12. Who supplied the Highlanders, who had been taken captive on board the *Annabelle*, with guns?
13. Who envisaged an earth with jet-liners by the year 1320 where Shakespeare himself would produce *Hamlet* on television?
14. Who was Tavius?
15. After the defeat of their captors on board the *Annabelle* where did the Highlanders travel to safety?
16. Who became the champion of the fake King John after the disgrace of Sir Gilles Estram?
17. Name the three French Catholics who plotted the assassination of the Admiral de Coligny. Why did they want to kill the Sea Beggar?
18. Who was Salah ed-Din Yusuf?
19. How was the Doctor responsible for the Great Fire of London?
20. The last of the Jagaroth race came to Earth many millions of years ago. Why did they leave the planet?

The Adventures of the Fourth Doctor/4

1. Who rode the Time Winds?
2. Name three members of the Ark in Space and give their respective fates.
3. What is the Test of the Horda? Name the two people who submitted themselves to the test.
4. Why were the Tigellans forced to retreat underground?
5. Space Beacon Nerva was supposed to be manned by forty-three operatives; when the Doctor, Harry and Sarah Jane arrived there from Skaro only four survived. Name them. Why had the others died?
6. Name the two Humans infected by the Krynoid seed pods.
7. What chased the Doctor across Tulloch Moor?
8. Who was Sholakh?

9. Why was Hardin's research into tachyonics so important for the survival of the Argolin race?
10. Who was Tomas?
11. Name the Planet of Evil.
12. Which planet was encircled by six 'suns'?
13. What did Sutekh plan to do once free of his prison on Earth? Why?
14. What did the Starliner's Systems Files contain?
15. What was the Zero Point?
16. How were the Mandrels able to escape from the Eden projection?
17. Who was Teka's hero?
18. How did the Doctor and Erato deflect the neutron star which had been aimed at Chloris?
19. Who took over the running of the Sandminer after the disgrace of Uvanov?
20. What in reality were the holy relics of the Sevateem?

The Adventures of the Fifth Doctor/4

1. What happened to the Mara after its defeat by the Federation?
2. To save Mawdryn and his company from the curse of eternal life would have meant the end of the Doctor as a Time Lord. Why?
3. Why did the survey team headed by Sanders come to Deva Loka?
4. Name three of the captains in the race for Enlightenment.
5. Name the two space pirates encountered by the Doctor and Nyssa.
6. How many Urbankans were to be found on board Monarch's ship?
7. Who was the Doctor mistaken for by the crew when he arrived on board Captain Striker's ship?
8. Of the entire crew and passengers of Speedbird Concorde 192, which one did not succumb to Kalid's hypnotic powers?
9. Who was the 'Renegade'?
10. Whom did the High Council of Time Lords send to

rescue the fifth Doctor and his other selves from the Death Zone? How did they win his co-operation?

11. Where did the Doctor complete his recuperation after his regeneration at the Pharos Project?

12. How did the fifth Doctor escape from the Cybermen on Gallifrey?

13. What is the only way in which the Mara can manifest itself on Deva Loka?

14. Who stopped the computer countdown to jettison Terminus's second fuel tank?

15. What did Bigon and his colleagues intend to do after the destruction of Monarch?

16. Why did Lord President Borusa desire Rassilon's gift of immortality?

17. Who was Sir Gilles Estram?

18. What vision did Panna show the Doctor and Todd on Deva Loka?

19. Who did the Vanir first suspect the Doctor and Kari to be?

20. Who was Aris?

The Cybermen/2

1. What was the main power source of Captain Briggs's freighter?

2. Why was it necessary for the Cybermen who invaded the Moon Base to use Humans to operate the Gravitron?

3. The Cybermen have often used Humans to help them in their plans for conquest. Who betrayed his fellow man in (a) *The Invasion*; (b) *Revenge of the Cybermen*; (c) *Earthshock*?

4. How did the Doctor stun and then destroy the Cyberleader on board the TARDIS?

5. How did the Cybermen propose to end all life on Earth after the failure of their invasion of the mid-20th century?

6. Name Captain Briggs's navigator.

7. On which planet did the Cybermen establish their tombs?

8. Mondas was the sister planet of which other planet?

9. Name the photographer who helped the TARDIS crew in their battle with the Cybermen in *The Invasion*.
10. How did the Cybermen receive energy from Mondas?
11. What in reality were the space rodents on board the Wheel in Space?
12. Who wanted to rule the world, seeing it as 'weak, vulnerable, a mess of unco-ordinated and impossible ideals', and used the Cybermen to help him?
13. Who was Kaftan?
14. Name two of the Cybermen in *The Tenth Planet*.
15. Of which company was Tobias Vaughn the managing director?

The Adventures of the First Doctor/5

1. In which adventure did all the clocks and watches on board the TARDIS melt and distort?
2. Leaving the planet of the Sensorites in the 28th century, the TARDIS materialised in England in the 20th century – or so the Doctor claimed. Where in fact had the Ship landed?
3. Who saved Blossom Lefavre from the dastardly clutches of the evil Darcy Tranton?
4. What was Deadman's Secret Key?
5. Who was Captain Edal?
6. Vortis was originally a moonless world, but when the Doctor, Ian, Barbara and Vicki visited it, the planet possessed many satellites. Why?
7. Who murdered the last Keeper of the Conscience on Marinus?
8. Who ruled Xeros when the Doctor and his friends visited that planet?
9. Who were the 'Screamers'?
10. Gold was particularly abundant on Vortis. What unusual properties did it possess?
11. Vicki left the TARDIS crew to stay with Troilus with whom she was deeply in love. His sister, however, distrusted her, claiming that she was a sorceress. Who was his sister and what was her fate?

12. What was the Dancing Floor?
13. How did the Rills intend to procure power to enable themselves to leave the doomed planet on which they were stranded?
14. In their quest for the Keys of Marinus, how did the TARDIS crew travel to the locations of the Keys?
15. Name the leader of the Menoptera spearhead force which had come to reclaim their home world of Vortis.
16. On which planet was the Sagaro Sea?
17. With what weapons were Jano's guards armed?
18. Who took over command of the Space Ark when its Commander fell ill?
19. What was the Isop-tope?
20. What fate awaited anyone who managed to beat the Celestial Toymaker?

The Time Lords/3

1. After the death of Chancellor Goth and the supposed death of the Master, what story did Borusa put forward so as not to sully the respected name of the dead Chancellor?
2. The Time Lords adopted their policy of non-intervention after the Minyans destroyed Minyos, using the nuclear technology given to them by the Time Lords. What incident caused the Time Lords to foreswear violence forever?
3. When the Doctor's TARDIS was summoned back to Gallifrey in *Arc of Infinity*, it was only the third time that such a thing had happened. Why did the Time Lords recall the Doctor?
4. The Doctor's bio-data can only be found on Gallifrey. Who passed this information on to Omega and, in so doing, committed a treasonable offence?
5. Meeting him many years after their last meeting, the Doctor found his old teacher Borusa as head of the Prydonian chapter of Time Lords. In the two subsequent adventures set on Gallifrey Borusa had risen

even higher in Time Lord society. What offices did he hold in these two adventures?

6. The Doctor has often fought renegade Time Lords, but very few have ever returned to menace him again. Name two of them.
7. On which planet was Morbius executed? What was his manner of execution?
8. Name one person present at his execution.
9. The Meddling Monk attempted to change the course of Earth's history by ensuring that King Harold won the Battle of Hastings. Which other Time Lord has tried to change Earth's history?
10. What is Rassilon's Star?
11. Name the Captains of the Citadel Guards on Gallifrey in the first three adventures set on the Time Lords' planet.
12. What is the Panopticon?
13. Upon succeeding to the Presidency of the Time Lords the Doctor issued Borusa with very specific instructions for decoration of his presidential quarters. What were these instructions and what were the Doctor's reasons for giving them?
14. What is (a) the Coronet of Rassilon, and (b) the Ring of Rassilon?
15. Name four female Gallifreyans whom the Doctor has met.

The Adventures of the Third Doctor/5

1. How was the Keller Machine finally destroyed?
2. Name the brother of President Zarb of Inter Minor who plotted against him.
3. Who was the Adjudicator who came to settle the dispute between IMC and the colonists? What ruling did he give? What were his real reasons for coming to that planet?
4. How did Aggedor die?
5. Captured by the Draconians, the Doctor, Jo and the Master faced death for entering Draconian space. How did the Doctor extricate himself from this situation?

6. Alpha Centauri called for Federation troops to help quell the miners' revolt on Peladon. Who came in answer to his call?
7. Who was Hippias? How was he killed?
8. How did the Doctor counteract the Spiders' mental-energy blasts on Metebelis 3?
9. Who was Bellal?
10. Who became Chancellor of Peladon after the death of Ortron? Who was offered the job but turned it down?
11. The Doomsday Weapon was a supreme weapon capable of massive destruction. What is the visible sign in the sky of its having been used once before?
12. When Vorg's Scope broke down, how were all its exhibits saved from death and sent back to their home planets?
13. To effect successful time transferences scientist Whitaker of Operation Golden Age needed vast amounts of power Where did he tap this power from?
14. Who killed Hepesh?
15. What was the Devil's Hump?

The Adventures of the Fourth Doctor/5

1. What was Mettula Orionsis?
2. Name the home planet of Zargo, Camilla and Aukon.
3. Who was the leader of the rebels encountered by the Doctor and Leela in Megropolis One?
4. Who attempted to kill the Doctor on stage?
5. To which planet was the TARDIS supposedly en route when the Doctor decided to land on Earth after leaving Traken? Why did the Time Lord materialise on this planet?
6. How did Melkur enlist the aid of Kassia on Traken?
7. From where did the Fendahl skull draw its energy?
8. Name the outermost planet of the Morestrans' known Universe.
9. Who were the winged servants of Aukon?
10. Who were the gods of the Minyans?
11. Name the servants of Cessair of Diplos.

12. Who were Brock and Klout on Argolis?
13. Towards the end of *Warrior's Gate* the Zero Point began to collapse upon itself. Why?
14. Rorvik and his crew were unable to survive this collapse. How did the Doctor and Romana escape?
15. Who was Till?
16. How did the Doctor and Sarah Jane survive being locked inside a decompression chamber in Scotland?
17. Who was Tyrum?
18. The Doctor destroyed the Rutan mother ship with a makeshift laser. What did he use to focus the lighthouse beam?
19. How did the Doctor lure the Mandrels back into the Eden projection?
20. How was Melkur defeated on Traken?

The Key to Time/2

1. Arriving on Tara, the Doctor sent Romana off to find the fourth segment of the Key to Time. What did the Doctor do?
2. Who saved Romana from one of Tara's wild woodland beasts?
3. Who was the head of the Taran church who presided over the coronation of 'Prince Reynart'?
4. Name Prince Reynart's swordmaster.
5. Who was the surgeon-engineer of Count Grendel of Gracht?
6. Who were the Dryfoots?
7. For whom was the Doctor mistaken when he first arrived on Delta Three?
8. Name two of the Swampies on Delta Three at the time of the Doctor and Romana's visit to that satellite.
9. The Doctor, Romana and Rohm Dutt were sentenced to the Seventh Ritual of Death on Delta Three. What was it?
10. How did they escape from it?

11. How did the Doctor save himself from being consumed by Kroll on Delta Three?
12. Who was Shapp in *The Armageddon Factor*?
13. Name the chief surgeon on Atrios and the beloved of Princess Astra.
14. The Black Guardian attempted to seize the assembled Key to Time by impersonating the White Guardian. How did the Doctor see through this disguise?
15. Once denied the Key to Time, how did the Black Guardian attempt to visit his revenge on the Doctor?

The Adventures of the Fifth Doctor/5

1. How did the Doctor defeat the Mara on Manussa?
2. How did he defeat it on Deva Loka?
3. Before the arrival of the TARDIS crew, what were the two forms of organic life on board Monarch's ship?
4. Who was the Federator's son on Manussa?
5. Name the captain of the Concorde which followed the original flight path of the vanished Speedbird Concorde 192.
6. From where did Borusa obtain the energy needed to activate the Timescoop and bring together the Doctor's different incarnations, his companions, and some of his old enemies?
7. Who was Chela?
8. Why was the Doctor unable to leave Mawdryn's ship with the Brigadier, Nyssa and Tegan?
9. Who were Kalistoran, Vaan and Mordaal?
10. What purpose did the Floral Chamber on board Monarch's ship serve?
11. Who won the race for Enlightenment?
12. Of which university was Professor Hayter a professor?
13. How did Hindle control the Kinda on Deva Loka?
14. Which empire succeeded the Manussan Empire?
15. Why did the High Council of Time Lords seek the Doctor's help in *The Five Doctors*?
16. How was Castrovalva destroyed?
17. Who led the Urbankans out of the Urbankan slime?

18. Name the manifestations of the Mara which Tegan encountered in her dream on Deva Loka.
19. Name Monarch's two colleagues whom the Doctor and his friends met.
20. Who led the TARDIS crew out of Castrovalva?

The Master/2

1. What solution did the Master and the Doctor come up with for grounding and neutralising the power of the Keller Machine?
2. Where on Gallifrey did the Master hide in *The Deadly Assassin*?
3. Why did the Master need the Xeraphin?
4. How did the Master convince George Trenchard to help him in his plans in *The Sea Devils*?
5. What ultimate plans did the Master have for the passengers and crew of the Concorde he had hijacked 140 million years ago?
6. How did the Doctor ensure that he would not lose track of the Master in *The Time Monster*?
7. What disguise did the Master's TARDIS assume in (a) *Castrovalva*; (b) *Time-Flight*; (c) *The King's Demons*?
8. How did the Doctor and Adric escape from the influence of the gravity bubble caused by the presence of the Master's TARDIS in *Logopolis*?
9. What power did the Master use to take over Tremas's body?
10. Whose body did he first intend to take over?
11. How did the Master escape from Xeriphas?
12. The Master intended to destroy the Doctor, Tegan and Nyssa by sending the Doctor's TARDIS back to Event One. What alternative plan did he adopt when the Doctor escaped from the Big Bang?
13. What did the Doctor use to damage the Master's TARDIS in such a way that the Master would find it extremely difficult to steer accurately at the end of *The King's Demons*?

14. On which planet did Chancellor Goth find the dying Master?
15. With which member of the TARDIS crew did the Master propose to enter an alliance in *Castrovalva*?

The Adventures of the Fourth Doctor/6

1. What is Robophobia? Name the two instances of it in *Robots of Death*.
2. Who tried to sell an alien nobleman a non-existent mine?
3. Why did the TARDIS come to Zeta Minor?
4. Who was Neman?
5. Returning to what they supposed to be Earth after the defeat of Sutekh, the TARDIS dematerialised, leaving the Doctor and Sarah Jane stranded. Why?
6. What was the ultimate fate of the Collector on Pluto?
7. How did Scarlioni enlist Romana's aid in perfecting his time machine?
8. What tale did the Kraals tell Guy Crayford to ensure his co-operation in their plans?
9. After the destruction of the transporter ship, how did the crew on board the Ark in Space return to Earth?
10. What was the cause of Mistfall on Alzarius?
11. What was the Underworld?
12. How did the Lady Adrasta die? Who attempted to seize power after her death?
13. Who came to the Sisterhood's aid when Morbius attacked their planet?
14. What did the Time Barrier on Leela's home world enclose?
15. Who was attempting to buy Argolis when the Doctor and Romana landed there?
16. How was the Zygon spacecraft on Earth destroyed?
17. Who was Kalmar?
18. What was the House of the Dragon?
19. How did Scaroth finance the time-travel experiments of Professor Kerensky?
20. Who was presumably the last Keeper of Traken?

General/3

1. What was (a) the Ark; (b) the Ark in Space?
2. Which two creatures encountered by the fourth Doctor are dependent on human blood?
3. Who was Damon in (a) *The Underwater Menace*; (b) *Arc of Infinity*?
4. What is Rondal?
5. Name (a) the Logician who awakened the Cybermen on Telos; (b) the squire of Edward of Wessex.
6. In which story did we first see the TARDIS's secondary control room?
7. Who was Doctor Foreman?
8. The Time Lords have often requested the Doctor's help, but he has only called on their help in three instances. Name them.
9. Who journeyed into the Black Hole and found the Eye of Harmony?
10. Who was (a) Princess Strella; (b) Princess Astra; (c) Princess Villagra?
11. Which race travels through time in dimensionally transcendental machines other than the Time Lords?
12. Which alien races encountered by the Doctor find heat particularly uncomfortable?
13. With whom did the Doctor have a swordfight in (a) *The Time Warrior*; (b) *The Androids of Tara*; (c) *The King's Demons*?
14. Name the journalist who (a) covered the Yeti invasion of London; (b) stowed away on the TARDIS; (c) was murdered by the Master on Gallifrey.
15. Several alien races have attempted to weaken or destroy Earth's population with deadly plagues or viruses. Name two of them.

1. Why was the Great Crystal of Knowledge so necessary for the Mara's Becoming on Manussa?
2. Which human was absorbed into the Xeraphin life force?
3. How did the Black Guardian hope to use the Eternals?
4. The Mara was 'destroyed' on Manussa 500 years before the Doctor's visit to that planet. Once every ten years a special festival was held to commemorate this event. What was so different about the final one of these festivals?
5. Who guided the Doctor and helped him to defeat the Mara on Manussa?
6. What did the Kinda wear as pendants around their necks?
7. What was so peculiar about Tegan's cabin on board Captain Striker's ship?
8. Who tried to escape from Monarch's ship in the TARDIS but only succeeded in materialising the craft some few feet away in space?
9. Why did Dojjen not destroy the Mara when the Great Crystal was in his possession?
10. Why can neither the Black nor the White Guardian totally destroy the other?
11. What was the bargain arrived at between Lon and Ambril on Manussa?
12. Who was Angela Clifford?
13. Why did Mawdryn return in the TARDIS to his ship rather than use his own transmat capsule?
14. Speedbird Concorde 192 was on a normal flight from New York to London when it disappeared. What happened to it?
15. Why did the Doctor finally agree to bring death to Mawdryn and his company?
16. Where did the Doctor promise to take Tegan after their adventure in 13th-century England?
17. How was the atmosphere on the top decks of the Eternals' ships maintained?
18. In whose keeping was the great Mind's Eye?

19. Who conspired with Borusa in his plan to gain immortality on Gallifrey?
20. Name the Doctor's two companions who accompanied his fifth incarnation to the Dark Tower.

Behind the Scenes

1. Which writers created (a) the Daleks; (b) the Cybermen; (c) the Yeti; (d) the Ice Warriors; (e) the Silurians and the Sea Devils?
2. Which actress who later played the role of one of the Doctor's companions was at first considered for the part of Susan Foreman?
3. Which famous British actor played the part of the Doctor in the two *Doctor Who and the Daleks* films?
4. On which two *Doctor Who* stories were the two Dalek films based?
5. Which *Doctor Who* story scripted by Robert Holmes was a vicious satire on the income-tax system in Britain?
6. In which story did William Hartnell as the Doctor turn to the camera and wish all his audience a Merry Christmas?
7. Until *The Savages* each episode of *Doctor Who* had its own title. Match the following episode titles with the overall title of the story to which they belong:

The Dead Planet	*The Massacre*
The Bell of Doom	*The Web Planet*
Escape to Danger	*The Chase*
The Waking Ally	*The Daleks*
The Bride of Sacrifice	*The Dalek Invasion of Earth*

The Death of Doctor Who *The Aztecs*

8. *Arc of Infinity* saw the return to the television series of the actors Michael Gough and Leonard Sachs. What roles did they play in this story? And what roles did they play in the earlier days of the series?
9. What actor who played the role of the Doctor has also played the part of a tragi-comic scarecrow?

10. Which *Doctor Who* story originally carried the title *The Day God Went Mad*?

11. Who played the role of the first Doctor in *The Five Doctors*?

12. The actor David Graham played the part of Professor Kerensky in the 1979 adventure *City of Death*. What more important role did he take in the William Hartnell days?

13. Four actors have played the role of Borusa. Name them.

14. Many actors have appeared several times in *Doctor Who*, each time playing different roles. Which roles have (a) Jean Marsh; (b) Nicholas Courtney played in the series?

15. Terry Nation is best known for his Dalek scripts. Which two other scripts has he written for *Doctor Who*?

THE ANSWERS

1. Earth.
2. Ian, who was made a knight by King Richard, and the Doctor, who was knighted by the fake King John.
3. The fail-safe mechanism materialises the TARDIS on board the nearest spacecraft. It was brought into use in *Terminus*.
4. Earth.
5. (a) The Shadow; (b) Turlough; (c) Captain Wrack. (Although Turlough's contract with the Black Guardian was only terminated at the end of *Enlightenment*, he can hardly be said to have been serving the Black Guardian in this story.)
6. Gallifreyans.
7. (a) Brother of Tuar who helped the Doctor fight the Spiders on Metebelis 3 until he was taken over by them; (b) Leader of the Vanir until he was replaced by Valgard.
8. (a) The Master's in *Castrovalva* and *Time-Flight*; (b) the Doctor's (the Doctor's chameleon circuit is now inoperative. However according to Susan it had assumed these two disguises before she and her grandfather met Ian and Barbara in Totter's Lane in 1963); (c) the Meddling Monk's in *The Dalek Master Plan*.
9. (a) The Master's TARDIS disguised itself as one in creating a complex dimensional trap for the Doctor and Adric in *Logopolis*; (b) The Doctor's TARDIS disguised itself as one to blend in with the London of 1963 – although a police box in a junk yard still seems a little out of place! (c) The Monk's TARDIS was briefly turned into a police box when the Doctor tampered with its chameleon circuit.
10. A space separate to our own, travel through which cuts down dramatically the journey time between interstellar bodies. Cessair's prison ship was stationed in hyperspace which Romana insisted was a theoretical absurdity!
11. Kasteroborous.
12. Space.

13. Slaar, Izlyr and Azaxyr.
14. (a) Samuel Pike's; (b) Captain Striker's; (c) Trask's.
15. The name given to the ancestors of the Daleks in the first Dalek story. According to Temmosus, in former times the Thals were the warrior race on Skaro, while the Dals were teachers and philosophers.
16. A situation in which two TARDISes occupy exactly the same position in time and space, causing the mutual destruction of the craft.
17. Skaro.
18. (a) Atrios; (b) Xeros; (c) Raaga; (d) Damos; (e) Vulcan.
19. Quad-magnetism which is given out by a Q-Star on burn-out. The force is highly unstable.
20. The weapon used by the Master which destroys people by imploding, or shrinking, them.

The Adventures of the First Doctor/1 – Page 12

1. Xeros.
2. In the 57th segment of time, some 10 million years into the future. The era of Nero, the Trojans and the Daleks took place in the first segment of time.
3. The coming of the Animus.
4. Earth.
5. Two years (the pilot of flight Red-Fifty was Steven).
6. In Fitzroy Square, London.
7. A slain Greek soldier and friend of Odysseus whose identity Steven assumed in Troy.
8. Ian was the only member of the crew who had drunk water taken from one of the aqueducts which had been poisoned by the company of insane Earthmen hiding in the caves on the Sense Sphere.
9. With electron guns.
10. Ian. Kala and Eyesen were the real culprits.
11. Kublai Khan's.
12. Because of his plans to make her enter into a marriage of convenience with Saladin's brother, Saphadin.
13. The Rills.

14. Kembel.
15. Achilles the Greek and Hector the Trojan.
16. Leon Colbert.
17. The Clanton brothers, Ike, Billy and Phineas.
18. Refusian spies.
19. They become his toys.
20. (a) He removed the dimensional control from the Monk's TARDIS, thereby causing the interior dimension to match the exterior dimension of the time machine; (b) he stole the Directional unit from the Monk's TARDIS.

Adventures in History/1 – page 13

1. The ejection into the void of one of Terminus's fuel tanks which then exploded, causing the biggest bang in history – Event One.
2. The explosion of the Jagaroth spacecraft some 400 million years ago, the radiation from which sparked off a chemical reaction in the amino acids on the planet.
3. The French Revolution.
4. Lord Palmerdale; Colonel Skinsdale; Adelaide; and Harker, the boat's coxswain.
5. Li H'sen Chang.
6. What they thought to be the trenches of the First World War. In fact, they had landed in one of the Time Zones on the War Chief's planet.
7. Charles Stuart, Bonnie Prince Charlie.
8. Cameca, the Aztec lady to whom he became engaged.
9. Horg.
10. Lemaitre, the governor of the Conciergerie Prison.
11. Because she saw the schoolteacher as a rival for Nero's affections.
12. Captain Avery's treasure. Avery was the former captain of Samuel Pike, Cherub and Joseph Longford.
13. Respectively, Wyatt Earp and Virgil Earp.
14. An atomic bazooka.
15. A wealthy merchant from Lydda. His wife and son were killed by the Emir and his eldest daughter Maimuna was

taken to El Akir's harem. He finally killed El Akir while rescuing Barbara from his harem and returned to his former life with Maimuna and his other daughter, Safiya.

16. In the Cave of Skulls. Old Mother released them on the condition that they would leave the Tribe, fearing, as she did, the secret of fire which they held. She realised that fire would bring destruction on the Tribe.

17. An actor fallen upon hard times who had become a highwayman. He helped the Doctor fight the Terileptils in the 17th century.

18. The day of the total eclipse of the sun in Mexico, on which day Tlotoxl performed an act of human sacrifice on the Perfect Victim.

19. Linx the Sontaran.

20. Krasis, the High Priest of the Temple of Poseidon.

The Adventures of the Second Doctor/1 – Page 14

1. Five hundred years.
2. On the Earth colony of Vulcan.
3. The computer of the Britannicus Ice Base.
4. Through activating a power booster on the TARDIS which took the time machine to Covent Garden underground station.
5. The Dynotrope, their spacecraft, had been damaged by enemy fire and they were forced to take emergency procedure and land on the nearest planet.
6. (a) Ta; (b) Lobos.
7. Tobias Vaughn.
8. *The Mind Robber*.
9. The Doctor.
10. Jamie, who then of course joined the TARDIS crew – promising to teach the Doctor how to play the bagpipes!
11. Toxic gas.
12. The Dulcians.
13. A founder member of the Britannicus Ice Base who left the base but later returned to help the Doctor and his former colleagues fight the Ice Warriors.

14. To find conclusive proof of the existence of the Yeti.
15. The Moon.
16. A nurse who helped the Doctor infiltrate the Chameleons' satellite. She too had originally been 'chameleonised' but her double was killed by a fellow Chameleon, posing as Meadows, an air-traffic controller.
17. The War Chief, a renegade Time Lord.
18. Navigator Rago and Probationer Toba.
19. Milo Clancey's.
20. He switched off the TARDIS's force field which enabled the organism sent by Omega to transport the police box and UNIT headquarters to the Universe of anti-matter.

The Daleks and the Thals/1 – Page 15

1. Davros foresaw a time of peace when all other life forms would have been suppressed by the Daleks. The Doctor realised that out of the Daleks' great evil some great good would surely come – many races who would normally have been enemies would unite and forget their differences to fight the Dalek menace.
2. On Spiridon in *Planet of the Daleks*.
3. (a) Carl Tyler; (b) Moni.
4. The Doctor. He was saved by the Kaled scientist Ronson.
5. Commander Sharrel; Agella; Lan.
6. The Thals' mutation went full circle until they evolved into the beautiful fair-haired humanoids encountered by the TARDIS crew. They established colonies and succeeded in fertilising small areas of land although they were greatly dependent on a great rainfall which occurred every four or five years.
7. Aridius; the Empire State Building; the *Marie Celeste*; a haunted house, an exhibit at the Festival of Ghana; Mechanus.
8. Trantis.
9. Peter Hamilton whose father was killed in the Dalek Wars, and Dan Galloway who lost his entire family.

10. Fifty years.
11. Antodus.
12. They manoeuvred the Dalek onto the insulated cloak which Alydon had given Susan. This cut the Dalek off from the static electricity in the metal floor on which it was dependent.
13. The Roboman died.
14. Dalekanium.
15. They discovered that Spiridon's icecanos were far too unstable for their use and so built their own massive refrigeration unit.
16. Mutos working for the Thals.
17. Radiation sickness.
18. Hensell. Bragen became Governor after ordering a Dalek to exterminate Hensell. After the rebel Valmar murdered Bragen to avenge the death of his girlfriend Janley, Quinn took over the running of the colony.
19. They subjected the Doctor to a mind-analysis machine.
20. Aridius.

The Adventures of the Third Doctor/1 – Page 17

1. Ashbridge Cottage Hospital.
2. Venusian Aiki-Do.
3. A resistance leader in the 22nd century who sent Anat, Boaz and Shura back in time to assassinate Sir Reginald Styles.
4. Because of the radiation emitted from the Doomsday Machine.
5. He believed the barrow to contain the tomb of a great warrior chieftain. In fact it contained Azal and his spacecraft.
6. From one of the satellites of the planet Grundle.
7. A Solonian chief who was used by the Marshal.
8. Ruth Ingram and Stuart Hyde (Professor Thascales was in truth the Master).
9. Ettis.
10. Earth and Draconia.

11. It is able to absorb, convert, transmit and programme all forms of energy.
12. It was made of ice.
13. A young Welsh Nobel prize winner (for his work on DNA synthesis) who established the Wholeweal community in Llanfairfach. He married Jo Grant.
14. The supreme leader of the giant spiders of Metebelis 3.
15. He made telepathic communication with the Time Lords who guided his TARDIS to Spiridon.
16. He was killed by a Sea Devil.
17. A guerilla sent back in time to kill the diplomat, but who disappeared back into the future before he could perform the deed.
18. Alpha Centauri who had met the Time Lord fifty years previously.
19. He believed that the two races could share the planet, with the Silurians inhabiting those dry and arid regions of the planet where Man did not live. He offered himself as a mediator in any possible talks between the two species.
20. The Nestenes.

The Earth in Danger/1 – Page 18

1. Four.
2. Stevens, the head of Global Chemicals who had been taken over by the computer. He was shown the error of his ways by the Doctor with the help of the blue crystal from Metebelis 3.
3. To persuade the Chinese to attend the meeting of world leaders at Auderley House.
4. The Old Silurian. He was killed by the Young Silurian.
5. Kenya.
6. Some 20,000–30,000 years ago.
7. By the fail-safe system.
8. By a freak accident in space in which his right hand was thrown clear of the detonation of his execution capsule and landed on the Earth of 150 million years ago.
9. The Daleks.

10. Twelve.
11. A mist in the streets of central London; the Great Intelligence's slowly moving Web in the tunnels of the London Underground; and, of course, the reappearance of the Yeti.
12. With web guns.
13. Giles Kent.
14. Harris.
15. Via the T-Mat system.
16. By blowing up sections of the London Underground.
17. By introducing a super-plague carried by rats.
18. General Finch.
19. Harrogate.
20. They were forced to return to their underground chambers faced with the threat of the cyclotron exploding. The Brigadier then blew up their caves, thereby sealing them up forever – much to the Doctor's disgust.

Companions of the Doctor/1 – Page 19

1. (a) Zoe; (b) Romana; (c) Polly; (d) Jo; (e) Tegan.
2. Ian.
3. Adric.
4. Because he was unable to take Sarah Jane to Gallifrey.
5. Ben and Polly.
6. The 25th.
7. Jo. She had been hypnotised by the Master.
8. Nyssa.
9. He was damaged by seawater when the Doctor and Romana took a holiday in Brighton.
10. Katarina.
11. To the Tomb of the Cybermen on Telos.
12. Polly. She was often called thus by Ben.
13. *Planet of Giants.*
14. Adric.
15. *The Aztecs.*
16. Susan, the Brigadier, Sarah Jane Smith, Tegan and Turlough, all of whom helped the Doctors on Gallifrey.

Also seen in the adventure were Benton, K9 and Romana, who was trapped with the fourth Doctor in the Time Vortex. Illusions of Jamie and Zoe, and Mike Yates and Liz Shaw were created to confound the second and third Doctors respectively as they made their way to the Tomb of Rassilon.

17. Respectively in *Horror of Fang Rock* and *The Brain of Morbius*.
18. Sole. He died submitting himself to the Test of the Horda in his daughter's place.
19. Turlough was to kill the Doctor, in return for which the Black Guardian would allow the boy to return home to his own planet.
20. Nyssa.

The Adventures of the Fourth Doctor/1 – Page 20

1. Skaro.
2. An ancient Druid goddess and one of the aliases of Cessair of Diplos.
3. The Vardans.
4. The Doctor and Sarah Jane used the Doctor's scarf to trip up the creature and he fell down a deep chasm. However, as the Doctor said at the time, silicon creatures are extremely difficult to kill and it is possible that Eldrad still lives.
5. Skaro.
6. A Movellan weapon capable of transforming the molecular structure of a planet's atmosphere in such a way that it becomes highly flammable. The Movellans intended to use it to destroy Skaro.
7. Mena.
8. The Inner Retinue.
9. He convinced Sutekh that the controls of the TARDIS were isomorphic and would only respond to his touch. In fact, the TARDIS can be operated by anybody.
10. Death.
11. Draith, Nefred and Garif. On Draith's death Login became a Decider.

12. The Nimon.
13. He used the TARDIS's Relative Dimensional Stabiliser to miniaturise the two clones and then injected them in the back of the Doctor's neck.
14. Vural.
15. Leela.
16. Because it contained the lump of jethrik which was the first segment of the Key to Time.
17. The Master in *Logopolis*.
18. Doctor Fendelman; Thea Ransome; Max Stael; Arthur Colby.
19. By the heat of the Sacred Flame which caused oxidisation of the minerals in the rock and, due to a chemical reaction with the super heated gases rising from the planet's core, formed the precious elixir.
20. A powerful laser tool, capable of punching a hole in thick armour-plating or 'removing the crystals from a snowflake one by one'. It was used by Taren Capel to make delicate adjustments on the brains of the Robots of Death and also in his attempt to burn out the Doctor's brain. Uvanov also used it to destroy V4 who was attempting to kill the Time Lord.

The Key to Time/1 – Page 21

1. So that no one person would possess the Key and the great power it contained.
2. The tracer with which the Doctor and Romana located the six segments of the Key and transformed them into their true forms.
3. Ribos. However they first located the segment on Cyrrhenis Minima; it was taken from that planet to Ribos by Garron.
4. Alliance Security Agents.
5. The Seeker.
6. Quartz. He needed the mineral to replace his Macromat Field Integrator.
7. The miniaturised husks of the planets he had plundered.
8. Queen Xanxia.

9. The planet Callufrax.
10. The Pirate Captain's right-hand man.
11. To Diplos, to preside over the trial of Cessair.
12. With tritium crystals.
13. Murder; the theft and misuse of the Great Seal of Diplos (in reality the third segment of the Key to Time); removing the Ogri from their home world; the detention of the prison ship in hyper-space; and the impersonation of a Celtic goddess, namely the Cailleach.
14. The Doctor interposed Cessair between himself and a Megara death ray. He then persuaded the Megara to probe Cessair's mind for damage and in doing so the justice machines discovered her true identity.
15. The stone circle on Boscombe Moor.

The Adventures of the Fifth Doctor/1 – Page 22

1. To help him recuperate from his regeneration. The Room is a part of the TARDIS shut off from the rest of the Universe and its healing properties are extraordinary.
2. Strictly speaking, Adric. The Master used the boy's mathematical skills in constructing the Block Transfer Computation necessary to bring Castrovalva into being.
3. Deva Loka.
4. A snake.
5. A surveillance device used by Monarch on board his ship.
6. A former Director of Manussa who became a Snakedancer and helped the Doctor to defeat the Mara on that planet.
7. Raaga, where they had worked in the tinclavic mines.
8. The Manussans created the Great Crystal some 800 years ago. However, they underestimated the extent to which the Crystal could absorb such emotions as fear and restlessness, and out of these emotions the Mara was brought into being.
9. An area in the Mountains of Gallifrey sealed off from the rest of the Time Lords' planet by an impenetrable

force field. The ancient Time Lords used it as a kind of gladiatorial arena in which kidnapped alien life forms (with the exception of the Daleks and the Cybermen, who were considered to be too dangerous) fought each other to the death for the Time Lords' amusement. It seems certain that Rassilon put an end to this barbaric practice, although one legend claims that he in fact instigated the Game.

10. Because of Monarch's having polluted the planet with his technology, the ozone layer was destroyed, so allowing ultra-violet light to scorch the planet's surface. Enlightenment falsely claimed that they had been forced to leave because their sun had turned super-nova.

11. Protein agglomerations created by the Master on prehistoric Earth.

12. By using the modified Metamorphic Symbiosis Generator which they had stolen from Gallifrey. The Generator did indeed give them immortality but also induced in them a perpetual mutation so horrible that the leaders of their planet sent them into eternal exile.

13. A colleague of Damon on Gallifrey. He was killed by Councillor Hedin using an impulse laser.

14. Slaves employed by Terminus Incorporated to oversee those afflicted with Lazars' Disease on Terminus and deliver them to the Garm. Their leader was Eirak who was succeeded by Valgard.

15. The librarian of the dwellings of Castrovalva.

16. In the Dark Tower in the Death Zone.

17. In a system of tunnels on Earth quite near to the Cybermen's deadly bomb.

18. As an aid for meditation in the Kinda's communal sharing of minds.

19. To the Great Exhibition of 1851 in Hyde Park.

20. The period when the Urbankans were still bound to their wholly physical bodies. As Enlightenment put it, 'the time of the chicken pox, hunger and heart disease, arthritis and the common cold'.

1. He proposed using Kamilion to stir up the Barons' hate for King John. Once the King had either been deposed or killed (with the throne of England possibly going to Philip of Spain), Magna Carta would never be signed at Runnymede and the whole course of British history (and by logical extension that of the entire world) would be undermined.

2. Fourteen. He has regenerated twelve times (giving him a total of thirteen different bodies) and on Traken took over the body of Tremas, Nyssa's father.

3. Chin-Lee.

4. The Master's TARDIS is a Mark Two model, a later model than the Doctor's, and as such the dematerialisation circuit was incompatible with the Doctor's TARDIS.

5. His Ogron slaves brought back the Doctor's TARDIS as part of the booty they had taken from an Earth cargo ship which they had raided.

6. (a) A special commissioner from Sirius Four; (b) the Portreeve; (c) an Adjudicator from Earth; (d) Sir Gilles Estram, the champion of the fake King John.

7. *The Daemons.*

8. In a fort on a small off-shore island. He escaped from his prison in *The Sea Devils.*

9. To penetrate the Sanctum of the Xeraphin to use the power within as a new energy source for his own TARDIS.

10. The discovery of the miniaturised corpses of Tegan's Aunt Vanessa and a policeman.

11. He planned to materialise the TARDIS underwater – and open the doors!

12. He interfered with the Logopolitans' computations to reconfigure the TARDIS and attempted to kill his enemy by miniaturising the time machine.

13. He picked it up when the Doctor accidentally dropped it in *The Mind of Evil.*

14. Through the Time Lords' files.

15. Xeriphas. The Doctor materialised his TARDIS at the same co-ordinates as the Master's TARDIS – but a few

seconds before. Both TARDISes were therefore unable to occupy the same space and the Master's TARDIS was sent back into time and space 'like a straight six into the pavilion'.

The Time Lords/1 – Page 24

1. The Doctor, of course; Susan; the Master; Romana; Omega; the Meddling Monk; Drax; K'anpo. A Time Lord also travelled to Earth to warn the Doctor of the Master's arrival on that planet in *Terror of the Autons*. Salyavin (Professor Chronotis) lived in Cambridge in the untelevised story *Shada*.
2. The Prydonian Chapter (the Doctor's chapter); the Arcalian Chapter; the Patrexes Chapter.
3. A stone tomb in the crypt in Amsterdam.
4. Just before the ceremony marking the resignation of the Time Lords' President.
5. The Doctor and Chancellor Goth.
6. To keep his other two unruly selves in order!
7. The Master interrupted the Matrix's prediction of the President's assassination and beamed it into the Doctor's mind, thereby luring his old enemy to Gallifrey.
8. In his previous visit to Gallifrey at the time of the Master's attempt to destroy his home world, he had stood as a presidential candidate to stay a sentence of execution which had been put on him. Upon Chancellor Goth's death, as the only other candidate he had become President by default.
9. Morbius. His brain, however, survived. The fourth Doctor was condemned to death on his first return to Gallifrey but claimed the immunity enjoyed by a presidential candidate. He was also condemned to death in his fifth incarnation but was saved by Hedin.
10. In a cave behind the Doctor's home in the mountains of South Gallifrey.
11. Through a fusion booster element, a highly advanced piece of equipment which was stolen from Gallifrey.
12. Mawdryn and his seven fellow scientists.

13. The Castellan.
14. The Time Lords removed the time machine's main space/time element.
15. Councillor Hedin.

The Adventures of the First Doctor/2 – Page 25

1. Mondas. It finally disintegrated when it absorbed too much energy from Earth.
2. A huntsman encountered by Ian, Barbara and Susan in their search for the third missing key of Marinus. He was killed by one of the Ice Soldiers who guarded the Key.
3. He planned to drop them off, regardless of where the TARDIS might next land.
4. They each wore Atmospheric Density Jackets.
5. The leader of the Saxon villagers attacked by Vikings in Northumbria in 1066.
6. They were accidentally transported to the Visians' planet when they interrupted an experiment in cellular transmission by the scientists Froyn and Rhynmal.
7. Reptilian creatures with one eye who had taken refuge on Earth from their own dying planet. They were the servants of the Guardians on the Space Ark and accompanied them to Refusis.
8. Jano was the leader of the Elders, Chal the leader of the Savages.
9. Malsan; Rynian; Prondyn.
10. In a dimension of dreams.
11. Vicki used her technical knowledge to open the locked arsenal on Xeros.
12. The door was obstructed by a girder which had crashed down in front of it.
13. The plain of the Pamir.
14. Between two crazy-paving stones.
15. Vicki's herbivorous pet. It was killed by Barbara who thought the creature was threatening the girl.
16. They wore acid-resistant wet suits and travelled underwater in glass submersibles.
17. John.

18. Bret Vyon. Vyon and Kert Gantry were sent to investigate the disappearance of Marc Cory on that planet six months previously.
19. In an ancient temple of light, built by the Menoptera to honour their dead.
20. At the South Pole.

Adventures in History/2 – Page 26

1. The 'Horse of Destruction', the Trojan Horse, the idea for which the first Doctor gave the Greeks.
2. The Silurians and their kin, the Sea Devils.
3. Irongron and his men.
4. Siberia in the 20th century. He believed he had been taken prisoner by the Russians.
5. By the Doctor taking Steven to the TARDIS where he was to be 'sacrificed'.
6. A black-magic sect in 15th-century San Martino, followers of the god Demnos. Their leader was Heironymous and they became possessed by Man-dragora.
7. (a) Samuel Pike's right-hand man; (b) the churchwarden who told the Doctor the secret location of Captain Avery's treasure; (c) a Cornish inn-keeper and smuggler who was finally killed by Cherub. Both Cherub and Longford were also former mates of the pirate Captain Avery.
8. *The Highlanders*.
9. A Chinese sect dedicated to the service of the god Weng-Chiang, whom they believed to have been incarnated in the person of Magnus Greel.
10. On the banks of the Orinoco in Brazil.
11. The Terileptils' ship.
12. Lord Ranulf and Lady Isabella of Fitzwilliam Castle.
13. The Minotaur.
14. Ian took the Doctor away into the bushes to 'execute' him and the two joined their companions, Vicki and Barbara, in the TARDIS.
15. The Meddling Monk, if we are to believe him! He

supplied the Ancient Britons with anti-gravity lifts to move the huge stones.

16. To avenge the murder of Reuben, their brother.
17. Napoleon Bonaparte.
18. He offered her a drink brewed from cocoa beans, unaware of the significance of this action.
19. The slave-traders who sold Ian and Barbara into slavery in the Rome of July AD 64.
20. *The Tribe of Gum* (which took place before the beginning of recorded history. Indeed, the TARDIS yearometer registered zero. *An Unearthly Child,* the first episode of this story, took place in 1963); *The Crusaders* (the time of the the Third Crusade, some time between 1190 and 1192); *The King's Demons* (1215); *The Massacre* (1572); *The Highlanders* (1746); *Black Orchid* (1925).

The Adventures of the Second Doctor/2 – Page 27

1. A kindly old gentleman who wrote 5,000 words a week on the adventures of Captain Jack Harkaway for the boys' magazine *The Ensign*. He was taken away from England by the Master Brain in the summer of 1926.
2. The Dominators.
3. A member of the colony threatened by the Macra who unsuccessfully tried to tell his comrades of the danger.
4. Commander Radnor.
5. The robotic servants of the Dominators.
6. Professor Zaroff. He proposed to do this by draining the ocean into the Earth's core.
7. A massive explosion would occur if the Ioniser were to be used at full power should the Ice Warriors' ship be nuclear-powered.
8. The Cybermen and the Cybermats (W3 LX88J was the Wheel in Space).
9. Lemuel Gulliver.
10. Because Earthmen were considered to be the most savage species in the galaxy.

11. By watching Astrid Ferrier piloting a helicopter in Australia. Needless to say, the Doctor was not a very competent pilot!
12. Mexican.
13. Orange sellers. They had used the money they had taken from Lieutenant Algernon Ffinch to buy the clothes.
14. By demolishing the supports of their Dynotrope.
15. *The Invasion*.
16. Three students taken on a tour of the Island of Death by Cully. They were killed by the Quarks.
17. Because the TARDIS's fluid links had broken, thus releasing poisonous mercury vapour into the atmosphere.
18. Fariah Neguib, his official food-taster.
19. With the use of Maxtible and Waterfield's time transporter.
20. Because the Doctor was the exact double of the would-be dictator, Salamander.

Companions of the Doctor/2 – Page 28

1. Susan and Romana (from Gallifrey); Leela; Adric (from Alzarius); Nyssa (from Traken); Turlough. The second version of K9 was constructed by the Doctor on board the TARDIS.
2. From being smelted in the Marshal's furnace.
3. Nyssa.
4. By means of a small crystal.
5. Marriner.
6. Romana.
7. Bret Vyon.
8. He saved the would-be dictator from a bomb attack which had been carefully staged by himself and Astrid Ferrier.
9. Jo. She assumed this identity on Peladon where only men of high rank and women of royal blood were allowed in the throne room.
10. To the Cornish coast in the 17th century.
11. Through the Ergon who probed the air hostess's mind.

12. Ostensibly because she had been sacked from her job with Air Australia. She had however undoubtedly longed to rejoin the crew ever since the TARDIS unexpectedly left her at Heathrow in *Time-Flight*.
13. Because he suspected her to be a time-sensitive, able to navigate his ship as could the Tharils.
14. To help cure Lazars' Disease.
15. Ben and Harry.
16. Dodo and Polly.
17. He condemned the boy to an eternal life of suffering on board Striker's ship.
18. He had injured himself while indulging in horse play on the Moon's surface.
19. Putting passengers on board a Concorde 140 million years in the past (see *Time-Flight*)!
20. Susan and Turlough.

The Cybermen/1 – Page 29

1. Mondas.
2. It was destroyed in the late 20th century when the energy it was absorbing from Earth became too much for it.
3. Because Earth was being host to an interplanetary conference with the intention of uniting to destroy the Cybermen. Even the Cybermen could not have withstood such an alliance.
4. The head of the Snowcap Tracking Station at the South Pole.
5. Captain Briggs.
6. He used Kellman to lure the Cybermen to Nerva; he then intended to destroy the Beacon with his Skystriker missile.
7. The Doctor used a matter transmitter to beam her down to the surface of Voga. This had the effect of ridding her body of the alien poison.
8. Two androids.
9. To attempt to recover the *Zeus Four* spacecraft.
10. Two hundred and fifty.
11. Voga, the planet of Gold.

12. He proposed firing the deadly Z-bomb at Mondas.
13. A Raston Warrior Robot.
14. The great number of dinosaur fossils in the caves.
15. Via the Cyberdirector.
16. Jules Benoit.
17. The disease was introduced in the Base's sugar stocks. Some members of the Base's personnel did not take sugar and so were not affected by the disease.
18. He intended to use the Cerebratron Mentor Machine which, among other things, was capable of generating emotional impulses to destroy the Cybermen. In the event of this plan's failure, he then intended to escape in the TARDIS.
19. Earth was in a state of red alert and a missile would therefore have been immediately detected by the planet's security systems.
20. They set Captain Briggs's freighter on a collision course with the planet.

The Adventures of the Third Doctor/2 – Page 30

1. The Doctor. Hepesh, the High Priest of Peladon, also had some success in taming the great beast until it turned against him and killed him.
2. To search for a certain species of giant toadstool which Cliff Jones hoped would solve the world's food problem.
3. Commander Stewart; Dan Galloway; Peter Hamilton; Jill Tarrant; Jack Railton.
4. To investigate the mysterious disappearance of top scientists and important scientific equipment.
5. Alpha Centauri.
6. By means of Skybase One's transmat system.
7. Fire.
8. Professor Kettering.
9. They believed the Doctor to be Sir Reginald Styles.
10. The Interplanetary Mining Corporation. They had come to the planet to mine for duralinium.
11. Captain Dent.
12. Arcturus. The Doctor was saved by Ssorg who destroyed the evil delegate.

13. By constructing a makeshift parachute-cum-balloon which caught the air current rising up a large ventilation shaft and brought them up to the surface of Spiridon.
14. Vorg's assistant on Inter Minor. She was formerly a member of the All-Star Dance Company.
15. Tuar, Arak and Rega.
16. From the Nuton power complex.
17. A member of the staff of the Wenley Moor atomic research centre who sided with the Silurians.
18. The local vicar, Mr Magister (in truth the Master).
19. General Williams.
20. It could clear and magnify the power of the mind.

The Daleks and the Thals/2 – Page 31

1. The Black Dalek Supreme.
2. The Daleks were unable to leave their metal city, dependent as they were on the static electricity which was transmitted up through the floor. Of the TARDIS crew Susan was the only one who was well enough to cross the jungle.
3. They hoped to be able to duplicate the Thal drug for their own use.
4. A Thal atomic shell which had destroyed his laboratory.
5. The Mechonoids.
6. The day on which the first full meeting of the Daleks' Grand Alliance of the 41st century took place.
7. With crude gun barrels and conventional ammunition.
8. They intended to use the natural fissures of the icecano to reach the heart of the Dalek City and plant bombs there to blow it up.
9. Ganatus.
10. With a rocket loaded with distronic explosives.
11. The guerillas Moni, Anat and Boaz. They regarded the Doctor as the only man who could possibly defeat the Daleks.
12. From the Lake of Mutations.
13. They had all been treated with the Thals' radiation drug which proved fatal to them.

14. Two Egyptian officers guarding the Great Pyramid on Earth who were exterminated by the Daleks.
15. By destroying the radio masts through which the Daleks communicated.
16. With explosive packs attached to six Daleks.
17. By sweeping the planet with a deadly space plague.
18. To study the secret of the Spiridons' invisibility.
19. (a) To replace the planet's core with a drive mechanism with which to steer it around the Universe; (b) to plunder the planet of its valuable minerals.
20. In each instance one member of the party impersonated a Dalek and pretended to be escorting its prisoners. Ian hid inside the Dalek casing on Skaro, Rebec hid inside one on Spiridon.

The Adventures of the Fourth Doctor/2 – Page 33

1. An alarm in the TARDIS signalling imminent danger to the time machine. It was first heard to sound in *Logopolis*, although an alarm system was in use in the TARDIS as early as *The Brink of Disaster*.
2. An astrologer at Lady Adrasta's court who displeased her and was flung into the Pit.
3. The Kraals.
4. In the star system of Tau Ceti (also the location of Ogros, the planet of the Ogri).
5. The TARDIS.
6. They were able to regenerate, a secret which had been passed on to them by the Time Lords.
7. By absorbing radiation from a nuclear reactor.
8. The expeditionary force which colonised the planet on which Leela would be born. The Doctor 'repaired' their malfunctioning computer – with disastrous results!
9. 400 million years ago in what has now become the Atlantic Ocean.
10. He placed a firework into the crevice from which the Flame issued. When the firework exploded, the soot caused by centuries of corrosion was dispersed and the Flame burned higher and brighter than before.

11. Head of the World Ecology Bureau in *Seeds of Doom*.
12. A scientist in the employment of Count Scarlioni. He died when Scarlioni turned the scientist's own time machine on to him, transforming him into a skeleton in a matter of seconds.
13. The more intelligent ones (such as Adric) became servants of the Three Who Rule; the remainder were fed to the Great Vampire.
14. He sent the TARDIS spinning off into space like a cricket ball, so that the planetoid did not destroy the time machine.
15. Taren Capel.
16. A Kaled general who had doubts about Davros's experiments and became a member of the group of Kaleds committed to investigating the production of the Daleks.
17. Tremas; Seron; Kassia; Katura; Luvic.
18. 'A fly caught by honey'.
19. Stor and a Sontaran trooper.
20. A poisonous barb used as a deadly weapon by the Sevateem. Its effect was to paralyse its victim and then slowly to kill him. The Doctor synthesised an antidote when Leela had been infected by one. Leela, however, continued to use the Thorns, much to the Doctor's annoyance.

The Adventures of the Fifth Doctor/2 Page – 34

1. Immortal beings who have power over matter and live outside time. Their own minds are wasted and empty, and they are dependent on the minds and imaginations of inferior beings for 'the sort of excitement which makes eternity bearable'. Eternals encountered by the TARDIS crew include Captains Wrack and Striker.
2. Beings who live within the bounds of time, as opposed to the Eternals who live outside time. The Doctor, as Captain Striker pointed out, is not an Ephemeral, but a Time Lord.
3. The former spacecraft used by Terminus Incorporated to cure people of the deadly Lazars' Disease.

4. Manussans who retired from society to lead a life of peace and contemplation in their attempts to reach the still point of their minds. The Snakedance was banned by the Federation some hundred years before the Doctor visited Manussa.

5. Their home planet was devastated by cross-fire in the Vardon-Kosnax war. Poisoned with radiation, they then melded themselves into a single unity in which shape they planned to rest until the contamination had passed and they could regenerate.

6. The Big Bang.

7. Adric.

8. (a) Princess Villagra; (b) Kurkutji; (c) Lin Futu.

9. In Andromeda.

10. Tegan.

11. Karuna.

12. A Kinda healing device, probably emitting sound at a level beyond normal hearing. It was used to put Hindle's mind back into phase after it had become unhinged.

13. He jettisoned part of the TARDIS to provide enough thrust to break away from the pull of Event One.

14. Sanders, the head of the expedition; Hindle, the Security Officer; Todd, the Science Officer. Roberts and two other members of the Dome disappeared on Deva Loka and were never met by the TARDIS crew.

15. In the Doctor's own mind.

16. The Doctor, who had been seriously injured after a malfunction of the transmat capsule.

17. An android capable of physical change, and used by former invaders of Xeriphas as a decoy. The Master used the android when he visited England in the early 13th century.

18. Ambril. Dojjen was his predecessor.

19. The Not-We.

20. An alias adopted by the Master when he was stranded on prehistoric Earth.

1. A device used by the Time Lords in cases of acute regenerative crises. Mawdryn and his company stole one from Gallifrey in their misguided attempt to become Time Lords.
2. Lord President Borusa and Chancellor Thalia.
3. Six minutes.
4. (c) Zorac. The Doctor and Borusa have both been President of the Time Lords.
5. The Master had promised Goth the Presidency of the Time Lords as, contrary to popular belief, the outgoing President had not named Goth as his successor.
6. *The War Games*; *Colony In Space*; *The Curse of Peladon*; *The Mutants*; *Frontier In Space/Planet of the Daleks*; *The Brain of Morbius*; *The Deadly Assassin*; *Arc of Infinity*.
7. To steal the Elixir of Life from the Sisters.
8. He attempted to hijack the Doctor's TARDIS.
9. Councillor Hedin.
10. That, although he had broken the Time Lords' rule of non-intervention, his actions had always been for good.
11. To deposit £300 in a London bank in 1968 and to travel 200 years in the future and collect the compound interest!
12. They are all member of the Prydonian Chapter – a Chapter well noted for its deviousness!
13. The third Doctor.
14. Chancellor Goth. The Doctor was at first suspected of the deed.
15. The Doctor. He did however appoint Chancellor Flavia his deputy and, as he later remarked, thereby made her probably the longest-serving Deputy President of the Time Lords in history.

The Adventures of the First Doctor/3 – Page 36

1. The Web City on Vortis.
2. At the South Pole.

3. The Drahvins. Of the Drahvins encountered by the Doctor, Steven and Vicki, only Maaga was a true Drahvin; the rest were clones.
4. The Elders, Jano's people.
5. The number-two scientist on the WOTAN protect who was enslaved by the machine.
6. With his ring.
7. By blowing up parts of their city which had been invaded by the Mire Beasts.
8. Aliases adopted by the Doctor, Dodo and Steven when they posed as a group of travelling players in the Wild West.
9. The former refuge of the Assassin murder cult, whose story was told by the Chinese girl Ping-Cho.
10. Susan.
11. Members of the escape chain with which the TARDIS crew became involved in 18th-century France.
12. Katarina.
13. Two of the Celestial Toymaker's toys.
14. Karlton.
15. (a) The leader of the Xeron rebels; (b) one of the Savages encountered by the TARDIS crew.
16. Liverpool.
17. He plunged over a cliff to his death on Dido when the sudden appearance of two Didonians startled him.
18. In the fourth Universe. As revealed in *The Edge of Destruction*, the Doctor and Susan almost lost the TARDIS on that planet some time before they met Ian and Barbara.
19. Via the Chumblies.
20. The Doctor.

Adventures in History/3 – Page 37

1. He took Sarah Jane to the present day and showed her the devastation Sutekh would visit upon Earth if they did not stop him in 1911.
2. Kirsty McLaren.
3. A gold bracelet. It became the means by which the

Animus on Vortis briefly controlled the schoolteacher.

4. Because of the failure of the assassination attempt on the Admiral de Coligny.

5. A young Chinese girl, a government official's daughter from Samarkand, who was travelling with Marco Polo to take part in her arranged marriage to an old man of high standing. She helped the TARDIS crew and became a particular friend of Susan.

6. A masque organised by Giuliano to celebrate his accession to the Dukedom of San Martino and to which he invited great men of learning. Mandragora hoped to turn this masque into a massacre and thereby check Earth's scientific progress.

7. Marco Polo.

8. Prince Henry of Navarre. He was spared lest his death should provoke a holy war.

9. The former fiancée of George Cranleigh, and Nyssa's double in the England of 1925.

10. Part of a control bracelet made from polygrite and used on prison planets such as Raaga to control difficult prisoners.

11. His suspicions were aroused by the King's lack of surprise at the materialisation of the TARDIS; and by the fact that King John was supposed to be in London on that particular day (4 March 1215) to take the Crusaders' oath.

12. Supposedly to discuss peace terms with the Khan on behalf of his leader Noghai; in reality, to assassinate the Khan.

13. Za. The Doctor exposed Kal as the murderer when, appealing to the savage's vanity, he made him produce his blade which was red with Old Mother's blood.

14. Troilus.

15. A Revenue officer encountered by the TARDIS crew in 17th-century Cornwall.

16. The collision of Captain Brigg's freighter ship (with Adric on board) with Earth. The collision caused millions of tons of rock and rubble to rise and fragment in the air, effectively blocking off the sun for months. The dinosaurs then died of hypothermia and starvation.

17. To give him an honour fitting and proper for the emissary of the King of England.
18. The Doctor, Tegan and Turlough; they were called thus by the fake King John. However, from the point of view of the real King John, the Master and Kamilion were the true Demons.
19. Linx.
20. (a) and (b). Although Catherine was a major character in *The Massacre,* she never actually met the Time Lord. In *The Masque of Mandragora*, the Doctor told Sarah Jane that he had never met Leonardo, and in *City of Death,* when he travelled back in time to 1505, he also missed meeting Leonardo. The Doctor met Nero and King Richard in *The Romans* and *The Crusaders*, and he revealed to Ian that he had met Pyrrho, the father of scepticism in *Sentence of Death*, the fifth episode of *The Keys of Marinus.*

The Adventures of the Second Doctor/3 – Page 38

1. He attempted to impersonate the Doctor and leave in the TARDIS.
2. Jarvis Bennet, the Station Controller; Doctor Gemma Corwyn; Leo Ryan; Zoe Herriet; Elton Lakeham; Enrico Casali; Bill Duggan; Armand Vallance; Kemel Rudkin; Tanya Lernov; Chang; Flannagan.
3. Jamie and Polly. The Doctor, because of his age, was put to work on the pump machinery on the surface.
4. The Chairman of the Refinery Board in *Fury From the Deep*.
5. At Edinburgh, under Lister.
6. A comic-strip hero, armed with an anti-molecular ray disintegrator, whom the Doctor and his friends met in the Land of Fiction. He appeared regularly in the Hourly Telepress of the year 2000 and was well-known to Zoe.
7. Alexander Denes was the Contoller, Nicholas Fedorin was his Deputy.
8. He had set up his laboratory in Atlantis.

9. Jamie with the aid of the Det-sen monks.
10. Senex.
11. Hermack.
12. He held her father, Dom Issigri, as a hostage.
13. By Jamie and Thomni's smashing its control pyramid in the Det-sen monastery.
14. The Doctor was sentenced to execution by firing squad; Zoe was sentenced to twenty years in a civilian prison; and Jamie, who was believed to be a Highland deserter, was to be returned to his regiment.
15. Ola.
16. The static electricity on which they were dependent on Vulcan (and indeed in their metal city on Skaro).
17. The Beacon was split up into separate sections by Caven. The TARDIS and its crew were at that time in two different sections of the Beacon.
18. Their brains were used by the Krotons and they were then vapourised.
19. The Abbot Songtsen; Khrisong; Thomni; Sapan; Rinchen; Ralpachan. Their master was Padmasambhava who had been taken over by the Great Intelligence.
20. One of the most expensive minerals in the galaxy and found only on planets far away from Earth. It is as incorruptible as gold and as strong as titanium, and was the main metal from which the space beacons were constructed.

UNIT – Page 39

1. Greyhound Leader.
2. Because of Ollis's mysterious disappearance. He had however been planning to contact UNIT for some time because of the streaks of 'space lightning' which he had detected.
3. Captain Munro.
4. The Silurians who were draining the power to awaken their fellows from hibernation.
5. Liz Shaw.
6. To investigate the destruction of North Sea oil rigs.

7. An American security agent sent by Washington to investigate the Master in *Claws of Axos*.
8. The liaison officer between UNIT and the regular army on *Spearhead From Space*.
9. Harry Sullivan. He posed as an inspector from the Ministry of Health.
10. With a machine constructed by UNIT's Sergeant Osgood, under the Doctor's instruction, designed to cool the air down in the heat barrier.
11. He believed that the Doctor's tinkering with his 'infernal machine' (the TARDIS) had caused his features to revert to those of his earlier incarnation.
12. To sort himself out after Operation Golden Age.
13. The Cybermen.
14. Major Beresford.
15. Mike Yates.
16. Liz Shaw.
17. Benton left the army in 1979 and became a secondhand-car salesman and Harry was seconded to NATO.
18. The traumatic shock of meeting his future self from 1983 on board Mawdryn's ship.
19. He suggested that Sir John Sudbury of Department C19 be contacted to verify status as a UNIT agent.
20. He became an A-level mathematics teacher at Brendon public school. He was also the commanding officer of the school corps, taught rugby and handled some administration.

General/2 – Page 40

1. The Abbot of Amboise and the Daleks' robot Doctor were both doubles of the first Doctor; Salamander was the second Doctor's double; the fourth Doctor met his android double in *The Android Invasion* and Meglos adopted the Time Lord's form on Tigella; the fifth Doctor's form was adopted by Omega during his second attempt to enter the Universe of matter.
2. Skaro.
3. (a) Xoanon; (b) WOTAN; (c) Mentalis.

4. (a) The owner of the circus where the Master first materialised; (b) a servant of Federico in San Martino.
5. (c) The Sontarans are the only species who are not invisible.
6. King Richard and King John (in truth, Kamilion).
7. (a) The Solonians in that stage of their natural mutation when their form was insectoid; (b) the mutated survivors of the war between the Kaleds and the Thals who were banished to the wastelands of Skaro.
8. A dreaded space leprosy, to which the only known cure is a massive dose of radiation.
9. It was destroyed by a Terileptil in *The Visitation*.
10. *The Horns of Nimon*.
11. A combination of an animal and a machine. The Skarasen was a Cyborg.
12. (a) Lakis; (b) Barbara; (c) Katarina.
13. Police Telephone Free for Use of Public. Advice and Assistance Obtainable Immediately. Officers and Cars Respond to Urgent Calls. Pull to Open.
14. (d) Mars. The Doctor has visited each of the other planets more than once, although, with the exception of Skaro, his earlier adventures on those planets have yet to be seen.
15. The Brigadier in *Mawdryn Undead*. Jo also met herself very briefly in *Day of the Daleks* when she returned from the 22nd century with the Doctor; and the Doctor, Ian, Barbara and Vicki also saw their future selves as exhibits in the Space Museum when the TARDIS jumped a time track.

The Adventures of the Third Doctor/3 – Page 41

1. The Image Reproduction Integrating System, a machine capable of translating thoughts into pictures. The Doctor used it on Professor Clegg as part of his studies into esp – with disastrous results.
2. A Federation miner who was struck down dead by the 'wrath of Aggedor'.
3. Captain Hart.

4. Channing. He was created by Hibbert.
5. A stone gargoyle brought to life by the Master's skill at psionic science.
6. It transformed Sergeant Benton into a baby, and Stuart Hyde into an old man.
7. The lower caste on Inter Minor used for menial work. At the time of Vorg and Shirna's visit to that planet they were showing signs of unrest and rebellion.
8. Anat.
9. Leeson and his wife Jane; Ashe and his daughter Mary; Winton; the Martins.
10. In the vicinity of the Nuton power complex, to enable it to draw on the power in the complex's reactor.
11. The official Earth delegate to Peladon.
12. Usually mutton, although they preferred human flesh.
13. Congressman Brook. He called for an out-and-out war with Draconia.
14. The engineer who came to Peladon to supervise the mining of trisilicate. He was in league with the Ice Warriors and was finally killed by Aggedor.
15. An intergalactic peep show containing miniaturised examples of various galactic life forms.
16. Whitaker's time machine which brought dinosaurs from the past into modern-day London. (In *The Five Doctors* it was the means Borusa used to bring the Doctors and some of their companions and enemies together in the Death Zone.)
17. The third Doctor. It was a name given to him by Miss Hawthorne in her attempt to persuade the villagers of Devil's End not to take his life.
18. Exarius.
19. Ortron.
20. By using the TARDIS to send the parasite into a Time Loop.

The Adventures of the Fourth Doctor/3 – Page 42

1. It was only through the Logopolitans' opening up of CVEs into other universes that the Universe could

survive when it had long since passed its natural point of heat death.

2. The talmar.

3. Two of the Outsiders, or Shobogans, encountered by Leela in the wastelands of Gallifrey and who helped defend the Citadel.

4. It was the sequence for checking the seals on a Skyfall Seven spacesuit. This was the Sevateem's only memory of being descended from an interplanetary survey team.

5. The Fendahl (or more precisely, the Fendahl Core, eleven fully grown Fendahleen and one embryo Fendahleen) was destroyed in the implosion of the Time Scanner. The Doctor destroyed the skull by dropping it into a supernova.

6. Descendants of the original crew of the P7E.

7. Because neither they nor their ancestors had ever come from that planet.

8. Six Mona Lisas, all painted by Leonardo – with the words 'This is a Fake' written on them in felt-tip pen by the Doctor in 1505.

9. Cassius (see *The Sunmakers*).

10. Reykjavik (see *The Talons of Weng-Chiang*).

11. The Supervoc SV7, the Vocs, the Dums, and D84, the robotic secret agent for the Company.

12. They were lured by Noah into a transporter ship which he then exploded in the deepness of space.

13. He disconnected the TARDIS's co-ordinated sub-system and took the time machine out of space and time.

14. Skinsdale gave Palmerdale secret advance information of the Government's financial plans which would have been to Palmerdale's advantage. In return, Palmerdale cleared Skinsdale of his gambling debts.

15. They believed that he could repair their malfunctioning android of Prince Reynart which they intended to use to thwart the plans of Count Grendel of Gracht.

16. With PCM (pento cyleinic-methyl-hydron) gas, an anxiety inducing agent which was pumped into the atmosphere of the Megropolises.

17. The androids, replicas of the staff at the Scientific Research Centre, were to take over the Centre, release

the Kraals' deadly virus and guide in the Kraal invasion fleet. They came to Earth in ejector pods from Guy Crayford's spaceship.

18. The original Keeper who summoned the Doctor and Adric to Traken; Kassia; Melkur (the Master); Luvic.
19. The Fendahl.
20. When he attempted to stop the creation of the Daleks on Skaro. He, of course, failed, but did manage to delay their progress by some thousand years.

The Daleks and the Thals/3 – Page 43

1. Mutos; the monsters in the Lake of Mutations; Varga plants; the Slyther; the Magneton (the metal beast discovered by the Doctor, Ian, Barbara and Susan in the petrified forest on Skaro); and the mutants created by Davros in his experiments.
2. He offered to show the Daleks the TARDIS if they let him and Susan go free. The Daleks refused, confident that they could find the time machine in the forest and learn how to operate it.
3. Theodore Maxtible.
4. She was put to work loading the nose cone of the Thal rocket aimed at the Kaled City with distronic explosives.
5. Light-wave sickness.
6. That he suspend work on the Daleks until a full investigation was carried out on them. After the destruction of the Kaled City, it was agreed that the work should be continued but only if conscience was restored to the Daleks.
7. He impersonated Zephon, one of the members of the Grand Alliance and attended the meeting in which the members of the Alliance discussed their plans.
8. Trantis. After the failure of this operation, he was exterminated by his Dalek 'allies'.
9. At the Chelsea heliport.
10. Barbara ordered the Robomen to destroy their Dalek masters and the Daleks were finally destroyed in the explosion caused by their own bomb.

11. He used a Dalek gun.
12. Mavic Chen's.
13. By giving the Thals the means to weaken the specially reinforced Kaled City dome, so that their own deadly rocket could penetrate. he betrayed his own people when they ordered a shut-down and an investigation of the production of the Daleks.
14. To travel back in time and to kill Sir Reginald Styles whom they believed to have been responsible for the World War, in the ensuing chaos of which the Daleks invaded and conquered Earth.
15. Bragen.
16. By releasing a deadly virus into the atmosphere which would destroy all those not immunised. The plan failed when the Spiridon Wester released the virus into the Dalek laboratory, forcing the Daleks who had not yet been immunised to seal off the laboratory forever.
17. They decided to bombard Skaro's atmosphere with radiation from their nuclear reactors.
18. They were defeated by their own weapon, the Time Destructor, which was activated by the Doctor.
19. Zoe.
20. *The Evil of the Daleks.*

The Adventures of the Fifth Doctor/3 – Page 45

1. As Captain Striker put it: 'The wisdom that knows all things and will enable me to achieve what I desire most.' For Turlough, it was the ultimate choice between good and evil.
2. Terminus.
3. The White and the Black Xeraphin encountered by the Doctor, Nyssa and Tegan.
4. The solar winds.
5. The first Federator, Lon's ancestor.
6. A mysterious being who helped to cure the Lazars on Terminus. He was under the control of the Vanir until the Doctor destroyed his control unit.
7. Entertainments held on board Monarch's ship as a rest

from work and representative of the different cultures on board that ship.

8. The destruction of the Universe.
9. One of Omega's attempts at psychosynthesis who helped him in Amsterdam.
10. His tapestry.
11. It used Tegan who was still under its influence to take the TARDIS to Manussa.
12. The site of Heathrow Airport 140 million years ago. The crew at first believed that they had arrived back at Heathrow in their own time.
13. Planets in Earth's solar system.
14. The White Guardian, who found it necessary to draw on the time machine's energy to contact the Doctor.
15. By telepathy, because, with the exception of Aris who had been taken over by the Mara, they were mute.
16. A means whereby an anti-matter creature can enter our Universe by assuming the body of a creature from the world of matter. Omega bonded with the Doctor in *Arc of Infinity*.
17. To travel faster than the speed of light in order to travel back in time before the Big Bang when he believed he would meet himself – God.
18. By strictly controlling the Vanir's supply of hydromel, the drug the Vanir needed to survive. The Company's hold over the Vanir was broken when Nyssa offered to synthesise the drug.
19. Enlightenment.
20. Through jewels which she presented to the captains or members of the other ships in the race for Enlightenment and through which she focussed the destructive power she could call upon.

Companions of the Doctor/3 – Page 46

1. K9.
2. By means of a sonic booster which fired a beam of ultrasonic sound at the android.
3. Tegan.

4. By connecting a circuit breaker to the Source Manipulator circuits which would destroy the Source.

5. An apparition believed by Jamie to appear before members of his clan before death. On the Moon, he believed a Cyberman to be the Piper.

6. Susan, as was seen most clearly in *The Sensorites*. All Time Lords are telepathic to some degree, so it seems reasonable to assume that Romana was also telepathic.

7. The White Guardian. Romana believed that the President of the Time Lords (who was presumably Borusa) had sent her.

8. She ejected herself and Kirksen, who was threatening her life, into space so that the Doctor would not give in to Kirksen's demands to be taken to the Daleks on Kembel.

9. Because she was asleep in the TARDIS.

10. Adric.

11. 28 Febuary 1981 (also the date on which the first episode of *Logopolis* was broadcast). Her flight was due to depart at 1730 hours.

12. Victoria.

13. The Drashigs. The Master's hypno-device, used in *Frontier in Space,* made one see the creature one feared the most. In Jo's case she saw a Drashig. She had not yet however encountered the giant maggots in Llanfairfach.

14. (a) Sarah Jane; (b) Jo; (c) Susan.

15. (i) In 1983 when he attempted to smash the Doctor's skull; (ii) in the TARDIS when he removed the TARDIS's main space-time element.

16. Sara Kingdom.

17. Susan at Coal Hill School.

18. (a) Jamie; (b) Victoria; (c) Vicki; (d) Sara Kingdom; (e) Katarina.

19. In *Four To Doomsday* he arrived presumably at the right time but in Monarch's ship, four days away from Earth; in *The Visitation* he arrived 300 years too early. He finally arrived at the correct destination in *Time-Flight,* and by accident!

20. When Turlough made the final choice between good and evil by freely choosing to save the Doctor from the Black

Guardian rather than accept the diamond which was his
right as the winner of the race for Enlightenment.

The Adventures of the First Doctor/4 – Page 47

1. In *The Dalek Master Plan* in the episode entitled
   Volcano.
2. The TARDIS in *The Myth Makers*.
3. The game to which the Celestial Toymaker challenged
   the Doctor and on whose outcome rested the fate of the
   TARDIS crew. It consisted of a triangular board and
   ten counters of varying sizes. The object of the game was
   to move the pile of counters from one corner of the
   board to another corner. Only one counter could be
   moved at a time, and a larger counter could never be
   placed on a smaller counter. The Doctor was required to
   complete the game in 1,023 moves.
4. It displayed on the scanner a series of photographs of a
   planet, a solar system, a galaxy and a blinding flash of
   light – the ultimate fate of the TARDIS crew if they
   could not halt the time machine.
5. Aridius.
6. Ian.
7. A new insecticide which threatened to alter drastically
   Earth's balance of nature.
8. 18th-century France during Robespierre's Reign of
   Terror.
9. So that the TARDIS crew could never arrive there in the
   future and become exhibits in the Museum, as they had
   seen in a terrifying vision of the future they experienced
   when the TARDIS jumped a time track.
10. In the Valley of Caves.
11. The Doctor, with some help from a Monoid.
12. By means of telepathic amplifiers which enhanced their
    natural telepathic power.
13. Dropping crystal stalagmites into Vortis's acid pools to
    feed the Animus and so enable it to spread its Web over
    the whole of Vortis.
14. The Menoptera, their own ancestors.

15. Hetra (their leader) and Nemini.
16. He surrounded the TARDIS with a force field, thereby
    stranding the crew on Marinus.
17. Marco Polo and his fellow travellers who included the
    Doctor, Susan, Ian and Barbara.
18. The captain of the *Marie Celeste* which was visited in
    rapid succession by the TARDIS crew and the Daleks.
19. She was hypnotised over the telephone. The Doctor
    used his large ring to bring the girl back to her senses.
20. Solar flares.

The Adventures of the Second Doctor/4 – Page 48

1. He was killed by the War Lord and his aides as he tried
   to escape in a Sidrat.
2. Swann.
3. He was murdered by Salamander when he discovered
   that Salamander had lied to him about the conditions
   above ground.
4. Padmasambhava.
5. By stabilising the Ioniser.
6. He used it to shield himself and the Gond Vana from the
   Krotons' dispersion unit.
7. Groups of people who refused to retreat from the
   encroaching glaciers during Earth's new Ice Age and
   preferred to eke out a primitive existence there.
8. Because of the radioactivity present there from the
   explosion of a nuclear bomb.
9. The Doctor and Zoe in *The Krotons*.
10. With sonic guns attached to their right forearms.
11. The Gorgon in the Land of Fiction.
12. Epsilon Four.
13. By destroying them with a neutron bomb.
14. The planetary crust there was extremely thin, making it
    an ideal place to drill through to the planet's core and
    tap the energy there to power their fleet.
15. The holy ghanta.
16. The Security Chief of the World Zones Authority.

17. The trenches of 1917; Roman Britain; the American Civil War in 1862.
18. T-Mat.
19. Ta in the Pliny solar system.
20. The servants of the Master Brain in the Land of Fiction.

The Earth in Danger/2 – Page 49

1. A festival held in that country in 1996. One of the exhibits there was Frankenstein's House of Horror, which was visited by the TARDIS crew and the Daleks. The event was closed because of serious developments in Peking.
2. The War Machine was immobilised within a magnetic field in Battersea.
3. Smithers.
4. Because he in fact instigated them.
5. It was built during the Second World War as a secret government base of operations.
6. Piccadilly Circus.
7. With a deadly poison which caused organic matter to shrink upon itself.
8. He proposed bombarding the area with nuclear warheads. The Doctor reversed the polarity of the neutron flow of a machine designed to reawaken the Sea Devils throughout the planet and so turned it into a bomb which destroyed the Sea Devils.
9. Colonel Alastair Gordon Lethbridge-Stewart.
10. With a deadly virus which, after destroying the Humans, would eventually burn itself out, leaving them free to colonise the planet.
11. The murder of the Commissioner of the Icelandic Alliance and his family by the Peking Homunculus in the 51st century.
12. In the heart of a hidden pyramid in Sekkara in Egypt.
13. It would have created a gigantic explosion, possibly destroying the planet.
14. It was only by using the Disintegrator Gun that the Giant Robot could break into the vault which contained the Destructor Codes.

15. Harrison Chase.

The Adventures of the Third Doctor/4 – Page 50

1. It was intended to reform hardened criminals by absorbing all the evil in their minds.
2. He won it off a Wallarian at the Great Wallarian Exhibition.
3. The Wholeweal Community, a group of idealistic young people in Llanfairfach researching into alternative lifestyles and technologies. Cliff Jones was one of their number.
4. Galaxy Five.
5. The box was intended for Ky. The Doctor attempted to discover the box's contents by using particle reversal, and met with some limited success.
6. Doctor Lawrence.
7. He drove the creature away with an iron trowel, a traditional defence against black magic.
8. The Nestenes are the evil creatures, a sort of cross between an octopus, a crab and a spider, who have control over the Autons, plastic creatures which are vaguely humanoid in shape and armed with wrist guns. The Replicas are a superior form of Auton designed to impersonate leading figures in the Government and, as such, are virtually indistinguishable from human beings.
9. Cotton.
10. Parrinium.
11. It was caused when General Williams fired upon a Draconian battle cruiser which he believed to be threatening his ship.
12. Alpha Centauri.
13. Jo Grant.
14. The Primitives; the High Priests; the Guardian of the Doomsday Weapon.
15. It was surrounded by a heat barrier.
16. Winton.
17. The TARDIS.
18. Humans (the crew of the SS *Bernice* and Jo); a Time

Lord (the Doctor); a plesiosaurus; the Drashigs;
Cybermen; Ogrons.
19. Professor Dale.
20. Because his mother had been an Earthwoman.

Adventures in history/4 – Page 51

1. Scaroth.
2. In a baker's shop in Pudding Lane.
3. Professor Litefoot. It had been given to his mother by
   the Chinese Emperor T'ungchi, after it had been stolen
   by bandits.
4. The official poisoner of Nero's court. Poppea ordered
   her to be thrown to the lions when she failed to poison
   Barbara.
5. King Priam.
6. El Akir. He actually captured the King's loyal servant,
   Sir William des Preaux, who deceived him into thinking
   he was King Richard. El Akir was also convinced for a
   time that Barbara was the Princess Joanna, Richard's
   sister.
7. The former first mate of the *Annabelle*, who betrayed
   his captain, Will Mackay, to the English and took over
   his ship which, in collusion with the crooked solicitor
   Grey, he used to transport prisoners to the West Indies.
   He was killed by Jamie.
8. Ian. He passed on the secret of fire to Za.
9. Leonardo da Vinci.
10. That of a page boy.
11. Wyatt and Virgil Earp and Doc Holliday.
12. The Doctor brought the guns which were then
    distributed by Ben, Polly and Kirsty.
13. The Meddling Monk.
14. The slave supervisor at the court of Nero. He was a
    Christian in league with Maximus Pettulian who
    planned to assassinate the Roman emperor.
15. To France.
16. The fifth Doctor.
17. Catherine di Medici, the Marshall Tavannes, the Abbot

of Amboise. The Sea Beggar was the leader of the main Huguenot faction opposing the Catholic heirarchy in France.
18. Saladin.
19. A burning brand was knocked from his hand by a Terileptil in the Terileptil Base in Pudding Lane, London.
20. Because it was unable to support life.

The Adventures of the Fourth Doctor/4 – Page 52

1. The Tharils.
2. Noah, who was taken over by the Wirrn, but finally succeeded in destroying them; Vira, who succeeded Noah as leader of the Ark; Lycett, who was absorbed by the Wirrn larvae; Libri, the Medtech whom Noah killed; Rogin, who was killed in the rocket blast from the transporter vessel carrying Noah and the Wirrn; and Dune in whose sleeping body the Wirrn Queen laid her eggs.
3. A means of determining guilt used by the Sevateem. It consisted of a pit filled with the carnivorous Horda, over which was placed a plank. The member of the tribe on trial would be required to stand on the plank and, with a crossbow, break a rope which would close shutters to the pit. Should he fail, the plank would break and he would be eaten alive by the Horda. Both Sole, Leela's father, and the Doctor took the test. Only one survived.
4. Because of the growing menace of their planet's aggressive flora.
5. Lester, Stevenson, Warner and Kellman. The other crew members had fallen victim to the virus introduced to the space beacon by the Cybermats.
6. Winlett, a scientist at the Antartica Camp Three; and Keeller, a fellow botanist of Harrison Chase.
7. The Skarasen.
8. The faithful lieutenant of the Graff Vynda Ka.
9. Hardin's experiments offered the Argolin their only chance of regeneration after they had been rendered sterile in their war with the Foamasi.

10. A member of the Sevateem who loved Leela. However, he refused to take the Test of the Horda in her stead, but did save her from death at the hands of Neeva's guards.
11. Zeta Minor.
12. Pluto.
13. To destroy all life in the Universe, lest some life form should arise which would threaten him.
14. Information on the history of the community on board the Starliner, and the Starliner's flight manual.
15. The intersection between the Universes of E-Space and N-Space.
16. The materialisation of the *Hecate* and the *Empress* into each other had created a dimensional instability, so allowing them to break free of their projection.
17. Seth.
18. The Doctor used the TARDIS's gravity tractor beam to slow down the approaching neutron star, so allowing Erato to surround it with an aluminium shield. This so minimised the star's gravitational pull that the Doctor was able to drag it off its course towards Chloris's sun. (The chances of this operation being successful were calculated at being 74,384,338 to 11 – which the Doctor claimed just happened to be his lucky number!)
19. Toos.
20. Relics from the survey team which had come to their planet many generations before.

The Adventures of the Fifth Doctor/4 – Page 53

1. It was banished to the 'dark places of the inside'.
2. It was only by using up the energies of his eight remaining regenerations that the Doctor could save Mawdryn and his fellow scientists. As Tegan said, what Mawdryn was asking of the Doctor was murder, eight times over.
3. To investigate the possibilities of colonising the planet. After the defeat of the Mara, Todd recommended that the planet was unsuitable for colonisation and that the Kinda should be left in peace.

4. Captains Striker, Wrack and Davy and Cretus the Greek.
5. Kari and Olvir.
6. Three billion.
7. The ship's cook.
8. Professor Hayter.
9. Omega in *Arc of Infinity*.
10. The Master. In return for his service they offered him a new regeneration cycle. (The Master had reached the end of his natural cycle of twelve regenerations, and it was only by possessing the body of Tremas on Traken that he was able to survive.)
11. Castrovalva.
12. He used the transmat device, given to the Master by the High Council, to transport himself to the Capitol.
13. Through the dreaming of an unshared mind.
14. The Garm.
15. To start a new life on another planet.
16. So that he could be the President of the Time Lords forever.
17. A French knight, the champion of the fake King John, and the Master's alias in 13th-century England.
18. A prophecy of the future as it would be if Aris's attack on the Dome succeeded; and a vision of the past chaos and decay caused by the Mara.
19. Spies for Terminus Incorporated.
20. A member of the Kinda and a 'father' of Karuna who was taken over by the Mara on Deva Loka.

The Cybermen/2 – Page 54

1. Anti-matter.
2. Because they were vulnerable to the gravity field generated by the Gravitron.
3. (a) Tobias Vaughn; (b) Kellman; (c) Ringway.
4. He stunned the Cyberleader by scraping Adric's badge for mathematical excellence which was rimmed with gold into the Cyberleader's chest unit. He then destroyed the Cyberleader with a Cybergun.
5. By detonating a Cyber megatron bomb.

6. Berger.
7. Telos.
8. Earth.
9. Isobel Watkins.
10. The energy was beamed directly to their helmets.
11. Cybermats.
12. Tobias Vaughn.
13. A member of the archaeological expedition to the Tombs of the Cybermen.
14. Shav; Krail; Krang; Talon; Jarl; Gern.
15. International Electromatics.

The Adventures of the First Doctor/5 – Page 55

1. *The Edge of Destruction.*
2. Outside Paris in 1794 during the Reign of Terror.
3. Steven, when the TARDIS briefly landed on a Hollywood set.
4. Deadman's secret key was Smallbeer, Ringwood, Gurney. This was the clue given to the Doctor by Joseph Longford which revealed the location of Captain Avery's buried treasure. The clue referred to names on the tombstones in the churchyard.
5. Captain of Jano's guards on the planet of the Elders and the Savages.
6. They had been drawn to the planet by the magnetic force of the Animus.
7. Yartek, the leader of the Voords.
8. The Moroks, whose leader on the planet was Lobos.
9. Bat-like creatures who inhabited Desperus, the Devil's planet.
10. It was a means whereby the Animus could exert its control over creatures on that planet.
11. Cassandra. She was taken by the Greeks during the Sack of Troy as a gift for Agamemnon.
12. A hall, at the end of which Steven and Dodo believed the TARDIS to be. The hall was filled with the Celestial Toymaker's dancing dolls, with whom Steven and Dodo only just escaped dancing for the rest of eternity.

13. They intended to draw on the energy from the core of the planet.
14. By travel dials which transported them instantaneously through space.
15. Captain Hilio.
16. Aridius. On the Doctor's visit to that planet, the sea had dried up and become a desert.
17. Light guns.
18. Zentos.
19. The Menoptera's Web Destructor which Barbara used to destroy the Animus.
20. Should the Toymaker be defeated, his world and everything in it would disappear – including the person who beat him. The Doctor got out of this impasse by pre-setting the TARDIS co-ordinates, and then imitating the Toymaker's voice to move the final piece of the Trilogic Game, rather than move the piece himself.

The Time Lords/3 – Page 56

1. That Goth had died in an exchange of staser fire after he had tracked down the Master who had assassinated the Time Lords' President.
2. Their terrible battle with the Vampires.
3. To terminate him and so prevent Omega from bonding with him and entering the Universe of matter.
4. Councillor Hedin, the Doctor's old friend.
5. Chancellor and Acting President, and then Lord President of the Time Lords.
6. The Master; the Meddling Monk; Omega.
7. Karn. He was vapoubised and his atoms scattered to the four winds of the Universe.
8. Maren, leader of the Sisterhood on Karn; Doctor Solon.
9. The Master, who hoped to prevent King John's signing of the Magna Carta.
10. The Eye of Harmony, the source of all Time Lord power.
11. Hildred (*The Deadly Assassin*); Andred (*The Invasion of Time*); Maxil (*Arc of Infinity*).

12. The great ceremonial hall on Gallifrey beneath which lies the Eye of Harmony.
13. That his quarters be redecorated entirely in lead. This was to shield his thoughts from the Vardans who can read minds.
14. (a) A jewelled coronet, capable of enhancing the power of one's will. Borusa used it to control the fifth Doctor on Gallifrey; (b) A ring which confers on whomsoever wears it the 'gift' of immortality – in reality a hideous living death throughout all eternity.
15. Susan; Romana; Rodan; Chancellors Thalia and Flavia.

The Adventures of the Third Doctor/5 – Page 57

1. It was consumed in the explosion from the Thunderbolt missile whose self-destruct mechanism the Doctor had operated.
2. Kalik.
3. The Master. He ruled in favour of IMC. His real reason for coming to the planet was to gain control of the Doomsday Weapon.
4. By a gun shot from Eckersley.
5. He revealed himself to be the mysterious stranger who had come to Draconia 500 years ago at the time of the 15th Emperor and had been created a Draconian nobleman for ridding the planet of a plague.
6. Azaxyr and his Ice Warriors.
7. The beloved of Lakis in ancient Atlantis. He was killed by the Minotaur while saving Jo in the labyrinth.
8. With stones he found on that planet which neutralised the effects of the Spiders' energy blasts.
9. An Exxilon who helped the Doctor on that planet.
10. Gebek, the miners' leader. The Doctor was first offered the job.
11. The Crab Nebula.
12. Through a link-up with the TARDIS.
13. From the nuclear reactor installed in the secret underground governmental base.

14. Aggedor.
15. A strange mound in the village of Devil's End containing Azal and his spaceship.

The Adventures of the Fourth Doctor/5 – Page 58

1. Traken's sun. It was blotted out forever when the Master interfered with the Logopolitan Program.
2. Earth.
3. Mandrel.
4. Li H'sen Chang.
5. Gallifrey. They changed course and materialised on Earth because of the Doctor's wish to make accurate measurements of a genuine police box (so as to help the Logopolitans repair the TARDIS's damaged chameleon circuit) and to avoid having to answer the Time Lords' awkward questions about Romana's decision to remain in E-Space to help the Tharils.
6. He promised that, in return for her service, her husband Tremas would not be taken away from her for ever to become the next Keeper of Traken.
7. From the energy released from Fendelman's Time Scanner when it disturbed the time fissure in the vicinity of Fetch Wood.
8. Zeta Minor.
9. Vampire bats.
10. The Time Lords.
11. The Ogri.
12. Members of the West Lodge of the Foamasi who had infiltrated the Leisure Hive posing as the real Brock and Klout, respectively an accountant and a lawyer on Earth.
13. Rorvik's Privateer was too massive, made as it was out of Dwarf Star Alloy. The collapse was accelerated when he attempted to destroy the mirrors by a back blast from his ship's engines.
14. Biroc helped the Time Lords to stay out of phase, thereby saving them from the destruction which enveloped Rorvik and his crew.

15. The manservant of Count Grendel of Gracht.
16. The Doctor hypnotised Sarah Jane and put her and
    himself into a form of suspended animation. They were
    eventually released from the decompression chamber by
    Benton.
17. The chief councillor on Voga.
18. One of Lord Palmerdale's diamonds.
19. By means of an ultrasonic dog whistle.
20. By the Doctor and Tremas invoking the Ultimate
    Sanction. This was a means whereby the five Consuls of
    Traken could cancel the Keeper's existence should they
    decide that he was unfit for the post. Normally this
    course of action required the consent of the five Consuls
    (and the use of their consular rings) and the Keeper
    himself, but after studying the plans of the Source
    Manipulator the Doctor devised a way of overriding
    these requirements.

The Key to Time/2 – Page 59

1. He went fishing.
2. Count Grendel of Gracht.
3. The Archimandrite.
4. Zadek.
5. Madame Lamia.
6. The Swampies' name for all those Humanoids not of
   their race.
7. Rohm Dutt the gun-runner.
8. Mensch; Varlik; Ranquin; Skart.
9. It consisted of being bound with creepers which
   contracted as the sun's heat dried them.
10. The Doctor succeeded in breaking a window through
    which rain came and caused the creepers to lengthen.
11. He used the tracer to transform the fourth segment of
    the Key to Time, hidden within Kroll's belly, to its true
    shape. Deprived of the power which had caused him to
    mutate to such an extraordinary size, Kroll vanished, to
    be replaced by thousands of tiny squid-like creatures.
12. The Marshal's assistant on Atrios.

13. Merak.
14. He realised the Black Guardian's true identity when he showed a total disregard for the life of Princess Astra, who was the sixth segment of the Key to Time.
15. He enlisted Turlough's aid to kill the Doctor.

The Adventures of the Fifth Doctor/5 – Page 60

1. He removed the Great Mind's Eye from its rightful place, the mouth of the snake carved on the wall of the Cave of the Mara. Once this was removed, the Mara was unable to channel the emotions of fear of the Manussans into itself.
2. By surrounding Aris with mirrors (taken from the Dome's solar generators); unable to face its own evil, the Mara was forced to recoil from itself.
3. The plants in the Floral Chamber and Monarch himself.
4. Lon.
5. Captain Stapley.
6. From the Eye of Harmony.
7. The assistant of Ambril on Manussa who helped the Doctor and Nyssa on that planet.
8. To escape from a temporal warp ellipse, it was necessary for the TARDIS to move either backwards or forwards in time as well as space to escape Mawdryn's ship. Nyssa and Tegan had been infected by Mawdryn and any movement into the past or the future would cause them either to revert to infancy and beyond or die of old age.
9. Three of the Dark Xeraphim called upon by Zarak.
10. To provide oxygen for Monarch.
11. The Doctor, aided by Turlough in *The Buccaneer*.
12. Darlington.
13. Through the use of mirrors which the Kinda believed had captured their souls.
14. The Sumaran Empire.
15. To investigate the power drain from the Eye of Harmony and the disappearance of two of their number inside the Death Zone. (Upon finding no trace of the Doctor in time and space, and discovering that the time

traces of four of his incarnations converged on the Death Zone, they requested the Master's assistance in rescuing the Doctors.)

16. By the destruction of the Master's Web and Adric's release from it.
17. Monarch.
18. Dukkha, Anicca and Anatta.
19. Enlightenment and Persuasion.
20. Adric.

The Master/2 – Page 61

1. They surrounded the machine in an electro-magnetic field.
2. In a forgotten chamber underneath the Capitol.
3. As a new energy source to replace the exhausted dynomorphic generator of his TARDIS.
4. He said that he was investigating the disappearance of several ships which he maintained were caused by enemies of England.
5. To use their bodies as a new source of protoplasm with which to make more Plasmatons.
6. He materialised his and the Master's TARDIS inside each other. Wherever the Master's TARDIS went, there would also go the Doctor's.
7. (a) A fireplace; (b) a Concorde; (c) an iron maiden. In (a) and (b) his TARDIS also assumed the familiar pillar shape as seen in *Logopolis*.
8. They rearranged the TARDIS's architectural configuration and jettisoned Romana's room.
9. The power he had gained from the Source through temporarily being Keeper of Traken.
10. The fourth Doctor's.
11. With the help of Kamilion.
12. Using the dimensional trap which was Castrovalva.
13. The Master's own Tissue Compression Eliminator.
14. Tersurus.
15. Adric.

1. An unnatural fear of robots. Poul, whom the Doctor and Leela met, was a robophobic, as was Zilda's brother who had died some time previously.
2. Garron.
3. In answer to a distress call.
4. The Proctor of Traken and the leader of the Fosters.
5. Having doubts about the location of the TARDIS's materialisation, the Doctor set the TARDIS onto pause control. The co-ordinates, however, were still set for Earth, and when Sarah Jane put the TARDIS key into its lock the pause control was cancelled and the TARDIS carried on to its original destination.
6. He wound up the Company's operations on Pluto, and reverted to his normal form, in which shape he was imprisoned by the Doctor.
7. He threatened to destroy Paris if she refused to co-operate.
8. He was told that the Kraals saved his life in deep space when his ship malfunctioned and Earth left him to die. They claimed to have repaired his shattered body, apart from his left eye which could not be found. In reality, nothing was wrong with his spacecraft, he had not been abandoned by Earth, and even his left eye, covered by an eyepatch, was complete.
9. Via the trans-mat beam.
10. A periodic shifting away of the planet from its sun. This was caused by the pull of another planet.
11. The warrens of innumerable tunnels and caves in the planet which had formed around the P7E.
12. She was crushed to death by Erato. Madame Karela then attempted to sieze power.
13. The Time Lords.
14. The spaceship in which the Mordee Expedition had come to that planet.
15. The West Lodge of the Foamasi.
16. The Doctor activated its self-destruct system.
17. A rebel scientist on the Great Vampire's planet in E-Space.

18. The temple and fortress of Magnus Greel prepared for him by the Tong of the Black Scorpion.
19. By the selling of priceless works of art which he had acquired and commissioned during his many lives.
20. Luvic. He became Keeper after the defeat of Melkur (the Master); shortly afterwards Traken was destroyed because of the Master's interference with the Logopolitan Program.

General/3 – Page 63

1. (a) The huge spacecraft carrying Humans, Monoids and specimens of Earth's flora and fauna to a new home on Refusis; (b) the former space beacon Nerva carrying Humans, and examples of the planet's flora and fauna, after the Earth had been evacuated because of the solar flares.
2. The Great Vampire and the Ogri.
3. (a) An Atlantean surgeon who became the leader of the survivors of Atlantis after the death of Professor Zaroff; (b) an old friend of the Doctor's who helped him on Gallifrey.
4. An intergalactic region devoid of stellar activity. It is the former location of a collapsed Q-Star and is also known as the Arc of Infinity.
5. (a) Eric Kleig; (b) Eric.
6. *The Masque of Mandragora*.
7. The name which Barbara and Ian mistakenly gave the Doctor on their first meeting, confusing him with I.M. Foreman, the owner of the junkyard at 76 Totter's Lane where they had discovered the TARDIS.
8. In *The War Games* when he needed their help to send all the captured Earth soldiers back to their respective periods of space and time; in *The Three Doctors* when he was being attacked by Omega's organism; and in *Frontier in Space* when he needed their help to follow the Daleks to Spiridon.
9. Rassilon.
10. (a) The first lady of Tara and the double of Romana's

first incarnation; (b) the princess of Atrios and the double of Romana's second incarnation; (c) the leader of the Mayans on board Monarch's ship.
11. The Daleks.
12. The Ice Warriors and the Rutans.
13. (a) Irongron; (b) Count Grendel; (c) Sir Gilles Estram.
14. (a) Harold Chorley; (b) Sarah Jane Smith; (c) Runcible.
15. The Daleks; the Silurians; the Kraals; the Terileptils.

The Adventures of the Fifth Doctor/6 – Page 64

1. The Crystal was the only means whereby the Mara could channel emotions of fear into itself and so manifest.
2. Professor Hayter.
3. Possessed of Enlightenment, he hoped that these creatures, who had no knowledge of good or evil would spread chaos throughout the Universe until it finally dissolved.
4. For the first time the true Great Crystal of Knowledge was placed into the serpent's mouth on the wall of the Cave of the Mara, thereby providing a means for the Mara to appear.
5. Dojjen.
6. A representation of the Double Helix.
7. It was a strange combination of her bedroom in Brisbane and her room on board the TARDIS.
8. Tegan.
9. Because it would have had no effect. The Mara can only be destroyed during its actual Becoming when it is between two modes of being, the physical and the mental planes.
10. To destroy one Guardian would also destroy the other, as neither Good nor Evil can exist without knowledge of the other.
11. Ambril agreed to give Lon the Great Crystal, in return for which Lon promised to tell the Director the location of valuable relics from the Sumaran Empire.
12. A stewardess on board the missing Speedbird Concorde 192.

13. His own transmat capsule was faulty, and in his much mutilated form it seemed unlikely that he could survive a return journey. The atmosphere in the TARDIS also helped his recovery.
14. It was thrown back in time 140 million years.
15. Because it was only by using the Metamorphic Symbiosis Generator to cure Mawdryn and his company that he could also cure Nyssa and Tegan who had been infected by Mawdryn.
16. To the Eye of Orion.
17. With an invisible energy barrier.
18. The Director's.
19. The Commander of the Citadel Guards.
20. Susan and Tegan.

Behind the Scenes – Page 65

1. (a) Terry Nation; (b) Kit Pedler; (c) Mervyn Haisman and Henry Lincoln; (d) Brian Hayles; (e) Malcolm Hulke.
2. Jackie Lane who played Dodo.
3. Peter Cushing.
4. On *The Daleks* and *The Dalek Invasion of Earth*.
5. *The Sunmakers*.
6. In *The Feast of Steven*, an episode of *The Dalek Master Plan* which was broadcast on Christmas Day, 1966.
7. *The Dead Planet* – *The Daleks*; *The Bell of Doom* – *The Massacre*; *Escape to Danger* – *The Web Planet*; *The Waking Ally* – *The Dalek Invasion of Earth*; *The Bride of Sacrifice* – *The Aztecs*; *The Death of Doctor Who* – *The Chase*.
8. In *Arc of Infinity* they played respectively Councillor Hedin and Lord President Borusa. They had previously played the roles of the Celestial Toymaker and the Admiral de Coligny.
9. Jon Pertwee who plays the part of Worzel Gummidge.
10. *The Face of Evil*.
11. Richard Hurndall.
12. He supplied many of the Dalek voices in the Hartnell

Dalek stories. He also played Charlie the barman in *The Gunfighters*.

13. Angus Mackay, John Arnott, Leonard Sachs, Philip Latham.
14. (a) Princess Joanna and Sara Kingdom; (b) Bret Vyon and the Brigadier.
15. *The Keys of Marinus* and *The Android Invasion*.

AUTHOR'S ACKNOWLEDGEMENTS

I would like to thank John Nathan-Turner, the BBC *Doctor Who* Office and Ian Levine for their invaluable help in the compiling of this book.

N.R.

DOCTOR WHO

0426114558	**TERRANCE DICKS** **Doctor Who and The** **Abominable Snowmen**	£1.35
0426200373	**Doctor Who and The** **Android Invasion**	£1.25
0426201086	**Doctor Who and The** **Androids of Tara**	£1.25
0426116313	**IAN MARTER** **Doctor Who and The** **Ark in Space**	£1.25
0426201043	**TERRANCE DICKS** **Doctor Who and The** **Armageddon Factor**	£1.25
0426112954	**Doctor Who and The** **Auton Invasion**	£1.50
0426116747	**Doctor Who and The** **Brain of Morbius**	£1.35
0426110250	**Doctor Who and The** **Carnival of Monsters**	£1.25
042611471X	**MALCOLM HULKE** **Doctor Who and** **The Cave Monsters**	£1.50
0426117034	**TERRANCE DICKS** **Doctor Who and The** **Claws of Axos**	£1.35
042620123X	**DAVID FISHER** **Doctor Who and The** **Creature from the Pit**	£1.25
0426113160	**DAVID WHITAKER** **Doctor Who and The Crusaders**	£1.50
0426200616	**BRIAN HAYLES** **Doctor Who and The Curse** **of Peladon**	£1.50
0426114639	**GERRY DAVIS** **Doctor Who and The Cybermen**	£1.50
0426113322	**BARRY LETTS** **Doctor Who and The Daemons**	£1.50

Prices are subject to alteration

DOCTOR WHO

	DAVID WHITAKER	
0426101103	**Doctor Who and The Daleks**	£1.50
	TERRANCE DICKS	
042611244X	**Doctor Who and The Dalek Invasion of Earth**	£1.25
0426103807	**Doctor Who and The Day of the Daleks**	£1.35
042620042X	**Doctor Who – Death to the Daleks**	£1.35
0426119657	**Doctor Who and The Deadly Assassin**	£1.25
0426200969	**Doctor Who and The Destiny of the Daleks**	£1.35
	MALCOLM HULKE	
0426108744	**Doctor Who and The Dinosaur Invasion**	£1.35
0426103726	**Doctor Who and The Doomsday Weapon**	£1.35
	IAN MARTER	
0426201464	**Doctor Who and The Enemy of the World**	£1.25
	TERRANCE DICKS	
0426200063	**Doctor Who and The Face of Evil**	£1.25
	ANDREW SMITH	
0426201507	**Doctor Who – Full Circle**	£1.35
	TERRANCE DICKS	
0426112601	**Doctor Who and The Genesis of the Daleks**	£1.35
0426112792	**Doctor Who and The Giant Robot**	£1.25
	MALCOLM HULKE	
0426115430	**Doctor Who and The Green Death**	£1.35

Prices are subject to alteration